BECOME A JUNIOR INVENTOR

CLOUD MENTOR

Illustrations by Kashmira Sarode

PUFFIN BOOKS

PUFFIN BOOKS
Published by the Penguin Group
Penguin Books India Pvt. Ltd, 7th Floor, Infinity Tower C, DLF Cyber City,
Gurgaon 122 002, Haryana, India
Penguin Group (USA) Inc., 375 Hudson Street, New York, New York 10014, USA
Penguin Group (Canada), 90 Eglinton Avenue East, Suite 700, Toronto, Ontario,
M4P 2Y3, Canada
Penguin Books Ltd, 80 Strand, London WC2R 0RL, England
Penguin Ireland, 25 St Stephen's Green, Dublin 2, Ireland (a division of Penguin Books Ltd)
Penguin Group (Australia), 707 Collins Street, Melbourne, Victoria 3008, Australia
Penguin Group (NZ), 67 Apollo Drive, Rosedale, Auckland 0632, New Zealand
Penguin Books (South Africa) (Pty) Ltd, Block D, Rosebank Office Park,
181 Jan Smuts Avenue, Parktown North, Johannesburg 2193, South Africa

Penguin Books Ltd, Registered Offices: 80 Strand, London WC2R 0RL, England

First published in Puffin by Penguin Books India 2015

Copyright © Cloud Mentor 2015
Illustrations copyright © Kashmira Sarode 2015

10 9 8 7 6 5 4 3 2 1

ISBN 9780143333029

Book design by Kashmira Sarode
Typeset in Museo by Kashmira Sarode
Printed at Replika Press Pvt. Ltd, India

A PENGUIN RANDOM HOUSE COMPANY

PUFFIN BOOKS
BECOME A JUNIOR INVENTOR

Cloud Mentor (www.cloudmentor.in) is a pioneering incubation platform for children that aims to nurture the inventors of tomorrow. Cloud Mentor's unique hands-on education program has been developed with years of meticulous research and classroom testing. It focuses on children building working models which combine both everyday material and technical components. The program has been developed with inputs from professionals working in STEM (Science, Technology, Engineering and Maths) and related careers. It aims to bridge the gap between industry and academia, theory and practice in a fun way. The Cloud Mentor Studio in Bangalore is a much-loved invention lab for kids where building any crazy contraption is always possible and usually happens every day!

This book has been written by Cloud Mentor co-founders, Nikhil Gumbhir and Vrunda Bansode, in close collaboration with their research and development team, ensuring that each activity in this book will work. Nikhil Gumbhir is an engineer by qualification and a mentor by choice. This book was directed by his rich hands-on experience in designing exciting, child-friendly content. Vrunda is passionate about creative, practical and meaningful education. She and the rest of the team have actively contributed to the concept design, activity testing and writing of the book.

With this book, the Cloud Mentor team hopes to inspire curious young brains to think differently—to imagine, build, engineer and invent!

CONTENTS

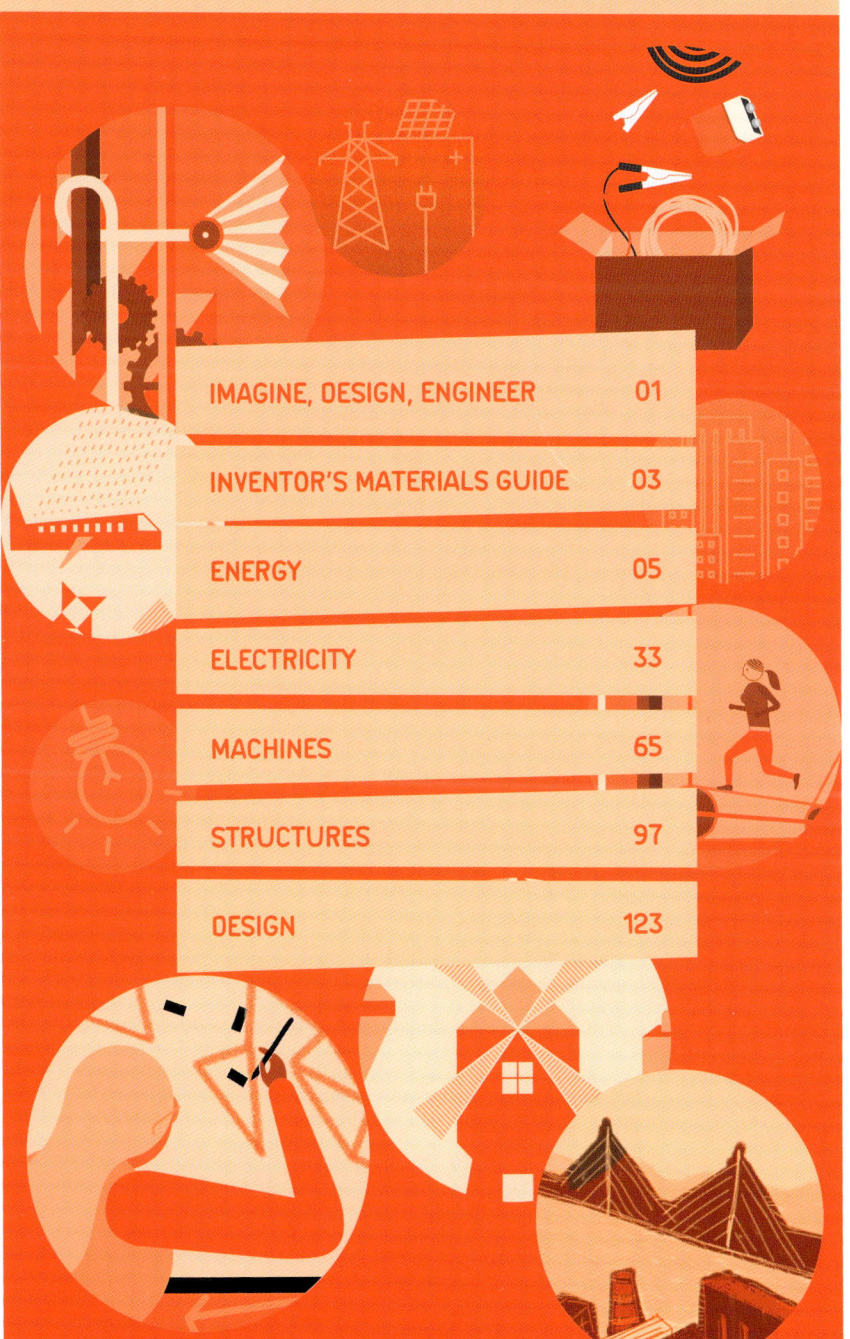

IMAGINE, DESIGN, ENGINEER!

'TO INVENT, YOU NEED A GOOD IMAGINATION AND A PILE OF JUNK.'

THOMAS EDISON

Who are inventors and what is invention? Haven't we all heard of Edison, Leonardo da Vinci, Tesla, Alexander Graham Bell and James Watt? They made new things or discovered better ways of doing something, that made our lives simpler and better. Think of electric lights, bicycles, trains, telephones—great inventions we cannot imagine our lives without! It is said that necessity is the mother of all invention and these creative minds solved problems and met needs with their ideas.

Inventions in today's era are not always about necessity alone, but also about making things and processes better. The Internet and email were not necessary for human existence, but haven't they completely changed our lives for the better? People like Bill Gates, Steve Jobs and even the engineers at Google can be called modern day inventors.

So what do all these people have in common? The spirit of curious investigation, fearless experimentation, creative thinking, lots of patience and perseverance! There is no standard path, degree or a textbook that teaches you how to invent something. The only way to become an inventor is to keep trying to be creative! And that's exactly what we will help you with in this book.

Apart from the inventive mindset, you also need some practical skills to be able to convert your ideas into reality. This book will introduce you to the basics of putting different things together to build a working model of a watermill or a roller coaster! You might face the same difficulties that real innovators face—material is difficult to find, connections are tricky to make and experiments may not work! Always remember that real inventors do not give up, they find better ways of making things work!

This book is divided into five sections:

ENERGY

This is what keeps the world going and it is important to understand what energy is before designing any working mechanism. This chapter takes you through some brain-tickling challenges on putting things together, helping you understand the different types of energy better.

ELECTRICITY

This is the most common form of energy we use in our daily lives. Most modern machines and gadgets work on electricity. In this chapter, you will learn to design and put together basic circuits and learn how these circuits can power up new appliances.

MACHINES

We depend heavily on machines for so much of our daily routine. It is fascinating to study and discover how a few common components can make huge, complex machines work! The Machines chapter will introduce you to the various simple machines and help you build awesome working gizmos of your own!

STRUCTURES

Designing and building better structures has always been important to inventors. Here, you will be introduced to new thoughts on architecture and building more comfortable, stronger and eco-friendly structures.

DESIGN

The all-encompassing idea of an entire invention is known as design, right from the necessity to the look, feel and user experience. The activities in the Design chapter will give you great opportunity to exercise and build your designing powers!

Armed with all these tools, what are we waiting for? Let's get creative, junior inventors!

How to use this book effectively:

- Form an Invention Team with your friends, parents and teachers.
- Keep collecting the required material as a team.
- Designate a school period or a day at home as a weekly Invention Day!
- Build your model on Invention Day and challenge your team to do more with brainstorm activities!

INVENTOR'S MATERIALS GUIDE

Most of the materials required for the activities in this book can easily be found at home (milk/juice cartons, wine corks, plastic bottle caps, etc.) or at a stationery/hobby store (Sello tape, glue sticks, paintbrushes, etc.) or at a convenience store (aluminium foil, straws, marshmallows, etc.). More specialized materials may need to be procured from a hardware store or a medical supplies store. A full list of these is below.

Materials from the hardware/ medical supplies store:

- Flexible PVC duct hose pipe
- Plastic syringes (Please discard the needles safely.)
- Plastic tubing (This needs to fit snugly on the plastic syringe hose)

Materials from the electrical shop:

- Roll of wire—this is thin metallic conducting wire in encased in insulating rubber covering on top. To make an electrical connection, you need to strip the wire ends. Peel away the rubber insulation to expose the metal wire inside.
- AA (1.5 V) batteries
- 9 Volt batteries
- 9 Volt battery snap—this fits onto the terminals of a 9 Volt battery and has two attached wires—red (positive) and black (negative) with stripped ends.
- Alligator or crocodile clips—these

are toothed clips on the ends of electrical wires.

- Bulb with wires—a small bulb with two attached wires with stripped ends
- Two-cell battery case—a holder for two AA batteries. The case should have 2 wires—red (positive) and black (negative) with their ends stripped.
- Light Emitting Diode (LED)—this has two leads: the shorter is negative and the longer is positive.
- Switch—this should have two attached wires with their ends stripped.
- Insulation tape—this is the tape used to seal the electrical connection made by twisting together the metallic ends of two wires. If the connection is left open, it may touch another metal wire/connection in the circuit causing a short circuit.
- Toy motor—a small motor with two attached wires with stripped ends.
- Toy propeller—a small plastic fan should fit snugly onto the shaft of the toy motor.
- Transistor (547 or 548)—this is an important electronic component. The number is visible on the flat side of the transistor.
- Copper and zinc strips
- Multimeter—this is an electronic measuring instrument that can measure electrical properties such voltage, current and resistance.

The full set of materials can be ordered at www.cloudmentor.in/juniorinventor

ENERGY

'Energy can neither be created nor
destroyed, it can only be changed
from one form to another.'
ALBERT EINSTEIN

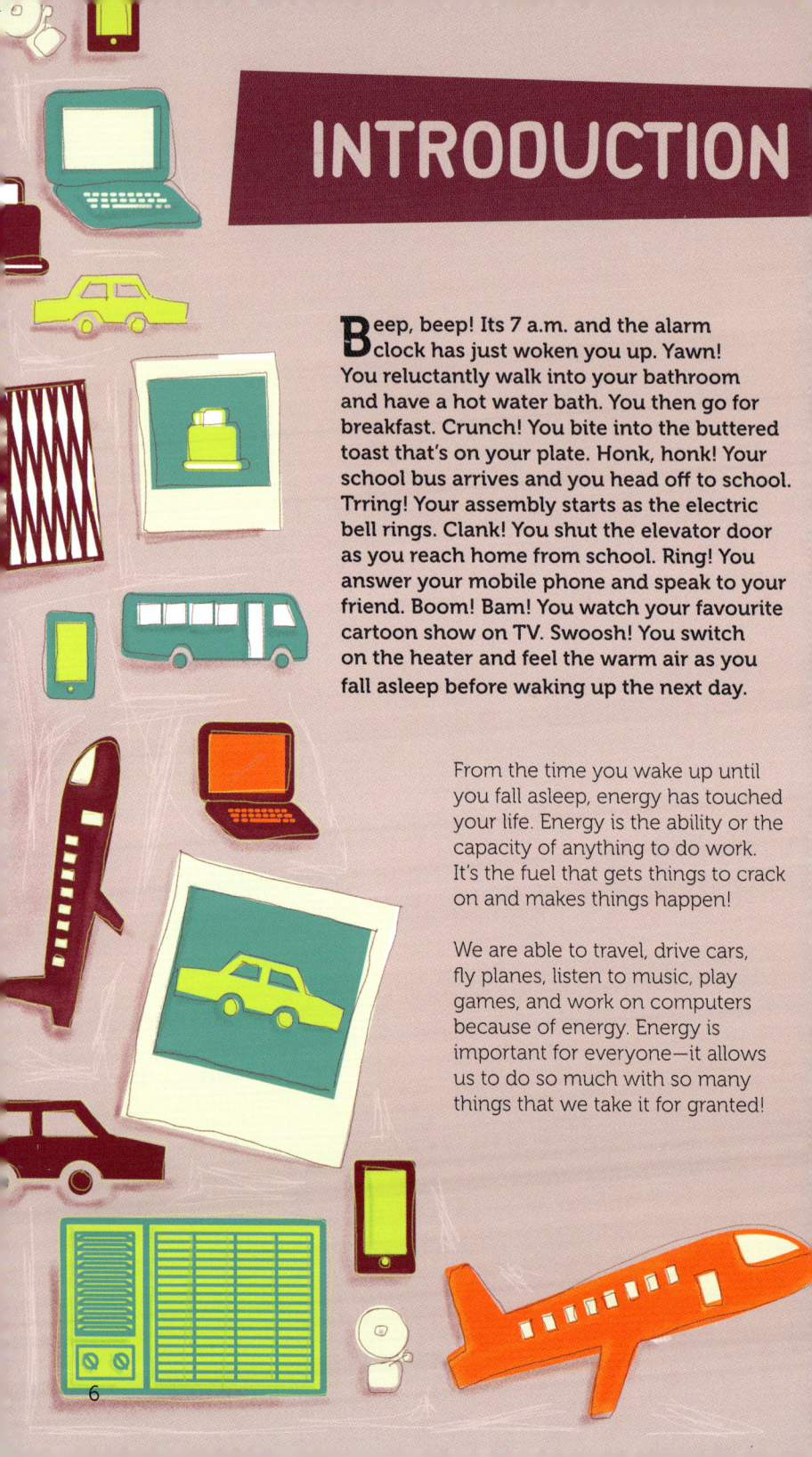

INTRODUCTION

Beep, beep! Its 7 a.m. and the alarm clock has just woken you up. Yawn! You reluctantly walk into your bathroom and have a hot water bath. You then go for breakfast. Crunch! You bite into the buttered toast that's on your plate. Honk, honk! Your school bus arrives and you head off to school. Trring! Your assembly starts as the electric bell rings. Clank! You shut the elevator door as you reach home from school. Ring! You answer your mobile phone and speak to your friend. Boom! Bam! You watch your favourite cartoon show on TV. Swoosh! You switch on the heater and feel the warm air as you fall asleep before waking up the next day.

From the time you wake up until you fall asleep, energy has touched your life. Energy is the ability or the capacity of anything to do work. It's the fuel that gets things to crack on and makes things happen!

We are able to travel, drive cars, fly planes, listen to music, play games, and work on computers because of energy. Energy is important for everyone—it allows us to do so much with so many things that we take it for granted!

ENERGY AND NEW INVENTIONS

NON-RENEWABLE ENERGY SOURCES

Coal

Oil

Fire

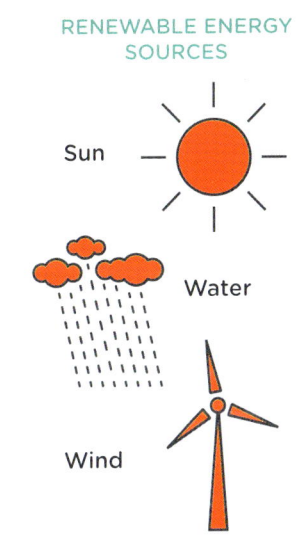

RENEWABLE ENERGY SOURCES

Sun

Water

Wind

Energy is a source of power for anything that exists, and for any new thing that we may want to invent. It can be harnessed from various sources and in various forms. The two main forms of energy are **potential energy** (energy that exists when things are static) and **kinetic energy** (energy that exists when things move). **Non-renewable energy** sources are sources that cannot be replenished or made again and will finish up in the time to come. Examples include fossil fuels such as coal, oil and natural gas. **Renewable energy** sources are those that can be replenished and constantly renewed. Examples include wind, sun and water.

When you start making inventions on your own, one of the most common problems you will encounter is powering up your invention and keeping it running for the maximum amount of time at the lowest possible cost.

Different inventions will need different amounts and different types of energy. It's up to you to choose your source of energy to keep your invention going. New inventions help the development of newer and better sources of energy. And so, inventing is a good thing!

THE ENERGETIC INVENTOR

Charles Francis Brush

He was an American pioneer in the commercial development of electricity. Brush contributed significantly to the development of the dynamo, arc lights and the wind turbine. He grew up on a farm with his eight siblings. Being the youngest, Charles probably did not have as many responsibilities on the farm as the others. Rather than waste his free time on trivial activity, Brush spent it reading about astronomy, chemistry, physics and other areas of science. However, he was not satisfied with only reading and started doing experiments in the workshop on his farm. When he was twelve, Brush constructed his first static electric machine, using a bottle, a piece of leather and amalgam from an old mirror. He also made batteries, electromagnets, induction coils and small motors. He was able to produce these devices from items on the farm. Brush could not afford expensive insulated wire but this did not deter him from making coils. He used rusty wire and shellacked paper to insulate the layers of wire. The rust on the wire, while not being an ideal insulator, provided enough insulation to make a functional coil. He later went on to become a great inventor, building upon the knowledge he had gained during his childhood years of tinkering with stuff around him.

WINDMILL

Anything that moves has a certain type of energy, be it a train, a car, electricity in wires or a steam engine. This type of energy is known as kinetic energy. Can you think of a natural source of kinetic energy? It's the wind! The movement of the wind has a lot of kinetic energy, which can be used to do mechanical work and generate electricity.

MATERIALS

1 thumbtack

1 cork, sliced into 3 pieces

1 knitting needle

1 one-litre juice carton

11cm
11cm

11cm
11cm

12 inches of thread

A 11-centimetre cardboard wind sail, folded as shown

INSTRUCTIONS

1

Place a piece of cork, then the wind sail and another piece of cork onto the knitting needle. Slide them all towards one end as shown.

2

Poke the pointed end of the needle through the carton and bring it out through the other side. Make sure the hole is big enough for the needle to rotate.

3

Put the third piece of cork on the pointed end. Push it in towards the carton. Tie the thumbtack to this end of the needle with the thread.

4

Blow on the wind sail and watch your thumbtack move up and down!

DID YOU KNOW

Windmills were developed as early as the ninth century as a more efficient method of grinding corn for making bread, providing an alternative to both animal power and water power. Persia and Europe were actively using windmills to pump water, grind grain and power factories. The Persian windmills had long vertical shafts with rectangle-shaped blades, whereas the early European windmills had horizontal shafts and were known as vertical windmills. Today, engineers are trying to design blades that can 'catch' as much energy from the wind as possible through a range of wind speeds. Blade design and engineering are the most important aspects of windmill technology.

PERSIAN WINDMILLS

EUROPEAN WINDMILL

Some things you can test and modify about your windmill blades include:

- Blade length
- Blade number
- Blade shape
- Blade materials
- Blade weight

Generating electricity is not the only application of wind energy, although it is the most common in the world today. Wind energy is also being utilized to run water pumps and vehicles! Traditionally, some modes of transport such as sailboats used wind as their primary energy source for movement. Just like the sail on the boats, some windmills have sail-like fabric on their blades to catch the wind.

Wind energy has become a popular source of clean, green energy globally. Huge wind farms with hundreds of windmills are being set up to maximize the utilization of wind energy.

Where do you think windmills should be erected? Very windy places where there are no tall structures around to obstruct the wind, right? Wind speed and the duration of strong winds determine the amount of electricity that gets generated. That is why it is important to choose a good windy spot to put up a windmill and to ensure that it catches maximum wind effectively.

BRAIN STORM

- Modify your windmill design so that it can lift a heavier object.

- Observe the working of the windmill after increasing the number of blades to 2, 3, 5 and 6 respectively.

TRIVIA

- One megawatt of wind energy = 2,600 fewer tons of carbon dioxide.

- A wind turbine blade can be up to 150 feet long, and a turbine tower can be over 250 feet tall, which is almost as tall as the Statue of Liberty!

ROLLER COASTER

Don't you love going to amusement parks? Aren't you crazy about roller coasters? Aren't you willing to stand in long queues just to get a ride on a roller coaster?

What is it about a roller coaster that gets us so excited? Is it simply the speed or is it the acceleration and the feeling of weightlessness? Let's figure it out!

MATERIALS

Double-sided tape

Marbles

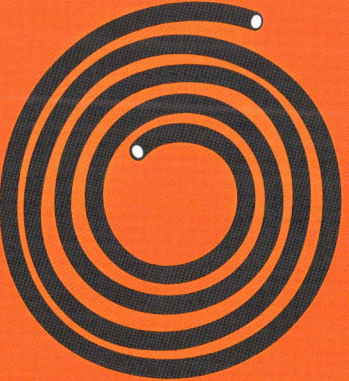

Flexible PVC duct hose pipe (10-12 feet long and 2 inches wide)

Scissors

INSTRUCTIONS

1

Cut the pipe in half through its entire length as shown.

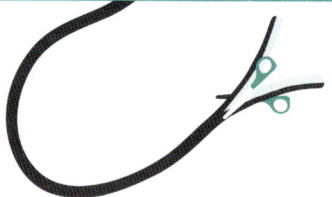

2

Tape one half of the pipe to the wall using pieces of double-sided tape creating the shape and a loop as shown.

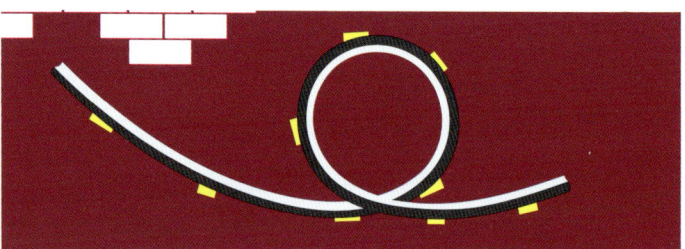

3

Line the inside of this pipe with double-sided tape (sticky side down, unpeeled yellow side up) to ensure that the marble rolls smoothly.

4

Drop the marble from the top end and watch your roller coaster in action!

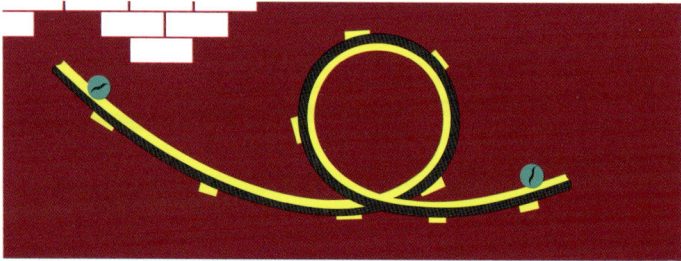

ROLLER COASTER

Up and down and down and up! Isn't it fun on the roller coaster? How does it keep moving? Have you ever played with toy car tracks where your car had to complete a vertical loop and speed towards the finish line?

Roller coasters work on the law of conservation of energy. This law states that energy can neither be created nor destroyed, it can only be transferred from one form to another.

Potential energy is the energy that an object has because of its height. Kinetic energy is energy an object has because of its motion.

A roller coaster does not have an engine to generate energy. The climb up the first hill is accomplished by a lift or cable that pulls the train up, this builds up a supply of potential energy. Once the train starts going downhill, this stored energy is converted into kinetic energy, which gets the train to move and scale the next hill. So, as the train travels up and down the hills, its energy is constantly shifting between potential and kinetic!

The highest hill in a roller coaster

is the starting point. If a taller hill was placed in the middle of the roller coaster, the train would not be able to go over because it would run out of energy.

Friction exists in all roller coasters and is caused by the rubbing of the train wheels against the track. Friction turns the useful potential and kinetic energy into wasteful heat energy. Friction is the reason roller coasters cannot keep going forever, so minimizing friction is one of the biggest challenges for roller coaster engineers.

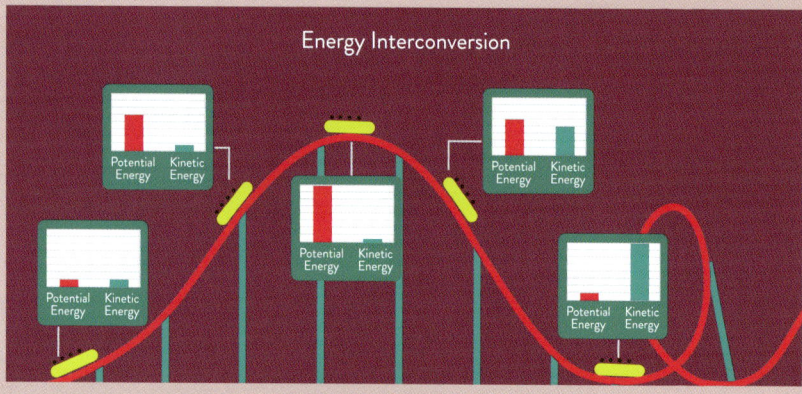

- Find a way of reducing friction in your roller coaster and try and make the marble roll for the longest possible time.

- Use marbles of different sizes and weights and observe the time and speed taken by each to reach the end.

- Use a longer pipe to make multiple loops in your roller coaster!

- We don't fall when we are upside down on a roller coaster because the force of acceleration counters the force of gravity!

SOLAR COOKER

What warms up a car when it's parked outside during the day? What causes our body to feel the heat when lying on a beach? What makes the wind blow and the ocean currents flow? That's right—the sun!

MATERIALS

Food to cook
(a slice of bread
with some cheese)

Scissors

A empty shoebox
with an attached lid

Plastic cling film

A glue stick

Black paint and
a paintbrush

Aluminium foil

2 straws

INSTRUCTIONS

1

Paint the outside of the box black.

2

Cut open a three-sided flap in the lid of the box, leaving an inch on all three sides as shown.

3

Use the glue stick to stick the aluminium foil as smoothly as possible on all the inside surfaces of the box as shown.

4

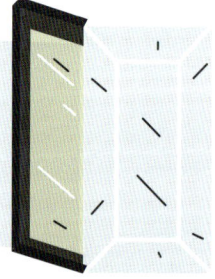

Open up the flap. Use the cling film on the inside and outside to tightly seal the opening on the box lid as shown. This will ensure that the hot air inside the box does not escape.

5

Use the two straws to prop the flap up. Preheat the box by placing it in the sunniest possible place.

6

After about half an hour, place your bread and cheese inside the box. Adjust the angle of the open flap such that the reflected sunlight falls on the food.

7

You now need to wait for your yummy food to get ready. It might take a bit longer depending on the sunlight but it will be worth the wait!

DID YOU KNOW?

Solar energy is the energy (light and heat) that comes from the sun. The sun is amazing and without it, there would be no life on earth. It rises every morning, gets our planet to wake up and sets at night. It's been doing this drill for the last five billion years! Every second, 600 million tons of hydrogen is converted to helium allowing the sun to practically be an infinite and powerful source of clean energy. Wouldn't it be wonderful to tap the sun's energy and use it to power up our daily lives?

Solar Energy

It is only recently that we have invented the solar panel and found easy ways to convert the sun's energy into the ever useful and important electricity!

Solar electric panels are made up of an element called silicon, which is the same thing that makes up sand. When sunlight hits a solar panel, it makes electrons in the silicon move around. The electrons flow through the built-in

Solar energy has always been existent. We have greatly progressed in the way we use solar energy to do useful work, right from using magnifying glasses to focus the sun's rays to light a fire, to constructing houses where the sun's energy could enter during winter, to adding glasses to windows to trap sunlight for heat, to creating a solar water heater that can boil water!

wires of the solar panel and electricity is generated! We can do whatever we want with this electricity—run a calculator, a music player, a traffic light, or, if we have big enough solar panels, even power up a satellite!

In our activity, we have used the sun's energy to cook food in the most eco-friendly way.

One of the many cool things about solar ovens is that they don't need electricity, gas, or wood to work. They cook food using only sunlight! Solar cookers are great because they save money and energy, and produce no pollution.

BRAIN STORM

- Modify your solar cooker such that it can heat water. Build a solar water heater.

- Paint the solar cooker with a different colour and observe the difference in the time taken to heat the food.

TRIVIA

- Solar panels are also called photovoltaic panels. Photo means light and voltaic means electricity.

SOLAR PANELS

WATERWHEEL

Have you ever gone white-water-rafting or taken a dip in the sea or crossed a river during a trek? Have you felt the enormous force of the gushing water?

Water makes up nearly seventy per cent of the earth's surface and is one of the easiest and cheapest sources of renewable energy! Let's try building a waterwheel to explore how we can convert the energy of moving water into other useful forms.

MATERIALS

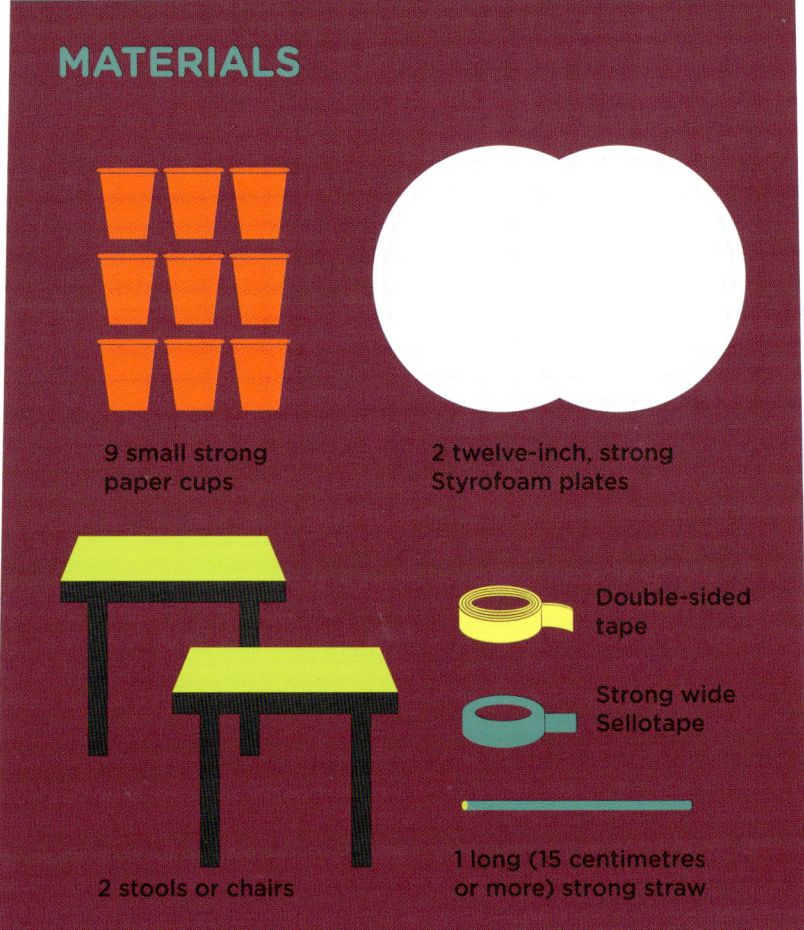

9 small strong paper cups

2 twelve-inch, strong Styrofoam plates

2 stools or chairs

Double-sided tape

Strong wide Sellotape

1 long (15 centimetres or more) strong straw

INSTRUCTIONS

1

Stick the Sellotape around the two plates making a wheel as shown.

2

Lay out a 3-foot long piece of double-sided tape with the sticky side up. Stick the cups three inches apart on this tape as shown.

3

Peel the other side of the tape and stick it over the Sellotape by winding it around the wheel.

4

Make a hole in the centre of the wheel and push the straw through it as shown.

5

Balance the straw over two tall stools. Pour water over the wheel and watch it spin!

DID YOU KNOW?

harnessed by human beings. The first waterwheels were used over 2000 years ago as mills to grind wheat into flour.

Placed under a source of water falling from a height, the buckets on the waterwheel would fill up, become heavy and move downwards, thus rotating the wheel. The same principle is used in the waterwheel that you just made!

The energy from flowing water can also be used to generate electricity. Dams are built to hold great reservoirs of water at a height, thus increasing the stored (potential) energy of the water. The greater the height of the water, the more is its capacity to generate electricity. It's similar to bouncing a ball from a height. The greater the height of the ball, the more it will bounce! The gates of these dams are opened periodically allowing the water to rush down at great speed, causing potential energy to be converted into kinetic energy. The gushing water flows through a turbine spinning it which in turn

WATERWHEEL

Hydropower is the oldest and cleanest method by which renewable energy has been activates a generator to produce electricity!

The future of harnessing hydropower would be from water that flows through our daily lives. Water flows at great speed from the overhead storage tanks, through our taps and showers. Rainwater also has a huge amount of kinetic energy, since it falls from a great height. Can you think of a way to harness this energy from rains?

DAM

BRAIN STORM

- Think of a way in which the energy from flushed out toilet waste water can be converted into electricity. Try drawing out your invention.

- Modify your waterwheel such that it can lift up a pin similar to the windmill activity.

TRIVIA

- The biggest and tallest dams in the world include the Rogun and Nurek dams in Tajikistan, the Xiaowan in China and the Tehri dam in India.

SODA BATTERY

Have you wondered what would happen if the world blacked out and all your batteries went dead? We have grown so used to electrical energy that we would be lost without it. Knowing how to produce your own electricity will help power some of the gadgets that you rely on every day.

MATERIALS

1 copper strip

1 zinc strip

1 small paper cup

1 bottle of any soft drink

1 electrical multimeter with attached red and black alligator clips

INSTRUCTIONS

1

Use the alligator clips to clip the copper and zinc strips separately to the inside of the paper cup as shown.

2

Pour the soda into the paper cup and ensure that the metal strips are submerged.

3

Set the multimeter to measure the electrical voltage as shown.

4

Your multimeter will display a number such as 1.06 or so to indicate the amount of electricity generated!

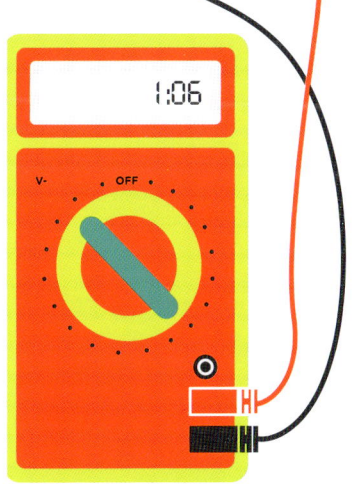

DID YOU KNOW?

was the **voltaic pile** invented by Volta in 1800. He put together a stack of discs of 2 different metals, adding brine (a solution of water/vinegar and salt) in between the metal layers. An electrochemical reaction in each three-disc unit of the pile formed an electric cell and generated a current!

In the battery we designed here, soda is the electrolyte and the copper and zinc strips work as the electrodes. In many developing countries, electricity is in short supply and is available only for a few hours a day. Home-made batteries can help people in such places as these batteries offer a cheap and alternative source of electricity.

Home-made batteries can be created using common items found around the house. Almost any fluid containing sufficient charged particles can serve as the electrolyte for a cell. It is possible to generate small amounts of electricity from

Electrochemistry is the branch of chemistry dealing with chemical reactions that involve electrical currents. Any battery has potential energy stored in the form of chemicals electrolyte (solution) and electrodes (positive and negative). This chemical energy is converted to electrical energy when the battery get connected to a circuit because electrons start moving rapidly from one electrode to another!

The first electrochemical cell

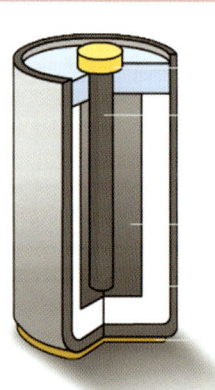

metal cap (+)

carbon rod
(positive electrode)

zinc case
(negative electrode)

manganese(IV) oxide

moist paste of
ammonium chloride
(electrolyte)

metal bottom (-)

Zinc Battery

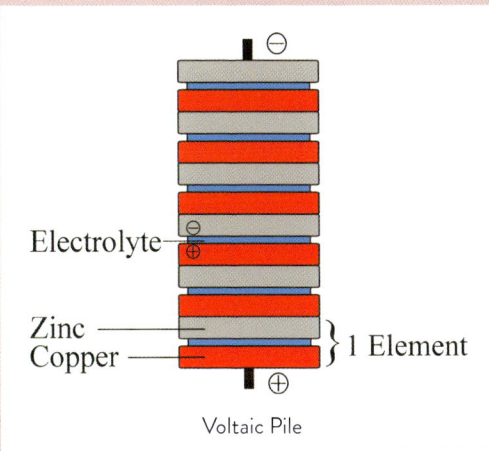

Electrolyte

Zinc
Copper

} 1 Element

Voltaic Pile

a lemon, potato, bleach or even a glass of saltwater!

UPS systems in homes and offices also have batteries in them that work on the principle of electrochemistry. The UPS battery has electrodes and an electrolyte that allows for the generation of electricity when the main power shuts down.

BRAIN STORM

- Try building a home-made battery by changing the electrolyte in the activity above to:
  a. Vegetable juice
  b. Saltwater
  Measure the amount of electricity that gets generated in each case.

- Make your own voltaic pile using two different types of coins and a salt-vinegar solution.

TRIVIA

- A multimeter is a device that is used to measure multiple parameters related to electricity. The first multimeter was invented by Donald Macadie, a British post office engineer.

THE FUTURE WORLD OF ENERGY

The world today is seriously looking for innovative, clean and renewable sources of energy. The conventional sources like coal, oil and other fossil fuels:
- Are about to run out
- Have become very expensive due to short supply
- Are polluting and hazardous

What do you think the future holds? How can we keep generating energy for an increasing population? How much will it cost? Are there ways in which we can generate energy locally instead of transporting it from far-off places?

PEDAL POWER

In search of newer sources of energy, we are trying to harvest energy out of every possible object and movement. You wouldn't believe some of these most innovative and eco-friendly sources of energy!

When you use your muscles to pedal your bicycle, muscle power gets converted to mechanical energy that moves your cycle forward. Can we use this movement energy to create or store some electrical energy? Of course we can—using a dynamo! A dynamo generates electricity by spinning magnets through a copper coil. A dynamo attached to the wheels of a moving bicycle can generate enough electricity to charge your mobile phone or music player or to even light up a headlight!

SOCCER BALLS

Kicking a football around is not just fun but can also be a useful source of energy! A portable generator inside the soccer ball can take all the kinetic energy that is generated from rolling around, convert and store it as electrical energy. With just a few minutes of play, this soccer ball generator can power up an LED lamp for hours!

BODY HEAT

Imagine being a walking power station! The heat that our body produces can be used to generate electricity in tiny amounts using a special device called a thermogenerator, which is a device that can convert heat into electricity. As an immediate application, this tiny output of power could be enough to power artificial organs such as a pacemaker. In the near future, we can expect a bigger breakthrough in generating more power through body heat. Thermo generators could be attached to clothing to allow gadgets such as mobile phones and wristwatches to be charged from human body heat!

PIEZOELECTRICITY

Do you know that walking, jumping and dancing can generate electricity? Piezoelectricity is the electricity resulting from pressure. Heavy traffic zones such as busy walkways and high impact floors such as dance floors have used piezo materials in their tiles to successfully generate electricity!

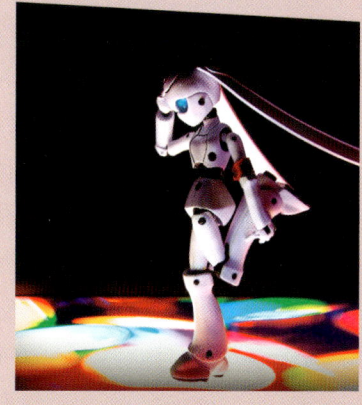

Piezoelectrics are a group of unusual materials—when you squeeze them, they make electricity! Material scientists are people who research on how strange materials work and help engineers find effective ways to use these materials. Pavegen piezoelectric tiles were successfully used in one of the busiest walkways into the 2012 London Olympic Games!

DESIGN THE FUTURE

Now that we know a little more about how energy can be found all around us and how we can harness it in innovative ways to make things work, how about designing your own invention combining various sources of energy?

BRAINSTORM

Imagine that it's 2025 and you've been chosen to design a smart house. Can you think of ways in which your house can be made more energy efficient? Use piezoelectric tiles, dynamos, windmills, solar panels, waterwheels and your own imagination! Design and draw your smart house here.

Electricity

'Electricity is really just organized lightning.'
GEORGE CARLIN

Let's imagine a world without electricity. Neither air conditioners nor fans exist, so you can say goodbye to sleep. You don't have a refrigerator to keep drinks cool or to preserve food. You can't watch the latest match or catch up on your favourite show because there is no TV. Oh wait, it doesn't matter—you have no time for entertainment, because you're too busy washing clothes, cleaning dishes and sweeping floors. There are no washing machines, dishwashers or vacuum cleaners to help you save time and energy. AND you can't do anything after sunset because it's too dark and there are no lights.

No electricity basically means that life as we know it wouldn't exist. Electricity is the most useful and the most common type of energy in our daily lives. It is a secondary source of energy, generated using primary or natural sources of energy such as sunlight, wind, coal, water, chemicals etc.

Electricity exists in different forms. Static electricity causes lightning during a thunderstorm. This is the same electricity that sometimes gives you a shock when you touch the handle of a car door.

Current electricity is the electricity that we use in our homes and offices. It consists of tiny charged balls that flow at great speeds through wires and power up all our

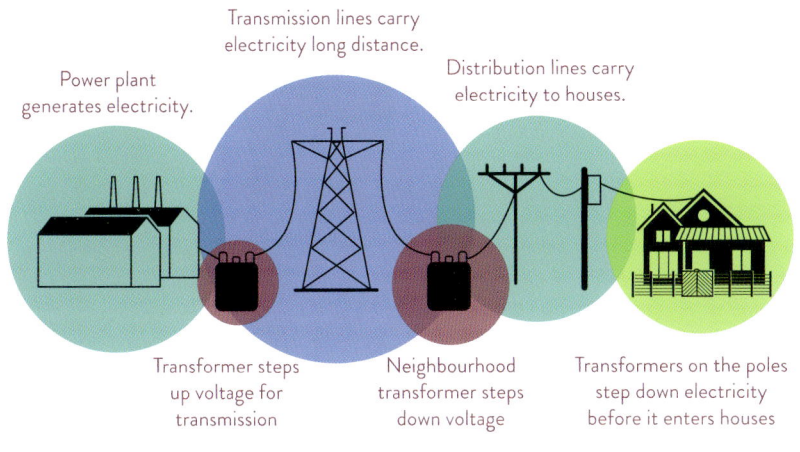

Power plant generates electricity.

Transmission lines carry electricity long distance.

Distribution lines carry electricity to houses.

Transformer steps up voltage for transmission

Neighbourhood transformer steps down voltage

Transformers on the poles step down electricity before it enters houses

devices. This electricity is generated in big power plants using magnets and copper coils. It travels through cables that you see along highways and roads to reach small gadgets like mobile phones as well as large machines like printing presses.

To utilize this flowing electricity effectively, we need to control and direct it by using electronic components like switches, transistors, resistors and sensors. These parts act like gates, speed breakers, accelerators and amplifiers and control the way the electricity flows and works. There is also an important safety safeguard in our household electric circuitry called a fuse. This protects us from electrical fires. A fuse shuts down the circuit system when there is a short circuit. During a short circuit, electricity takes a

shorter direct path between the positive and negative terminals of the power source and causes a fire. To prevent a short circuit, we need to ensure that no two wires in a circuit are unnecessarily touching each other. This is why all wires have an insulated material encasing them. In the activities in this chapter, you will use insulation tape on the connections to prevent a short circuit. If the battery gets short circuited, electrons flow very quickly from the battery through the circuit. This heats up the battery and the circuit and causes the battery to drain out.

Once you get to know these basic components and their functions, you can design and create a circuit to make electricity do whatever you want! Are you ready, Junior Inventors?

THE ELECTRIC INVENTOR

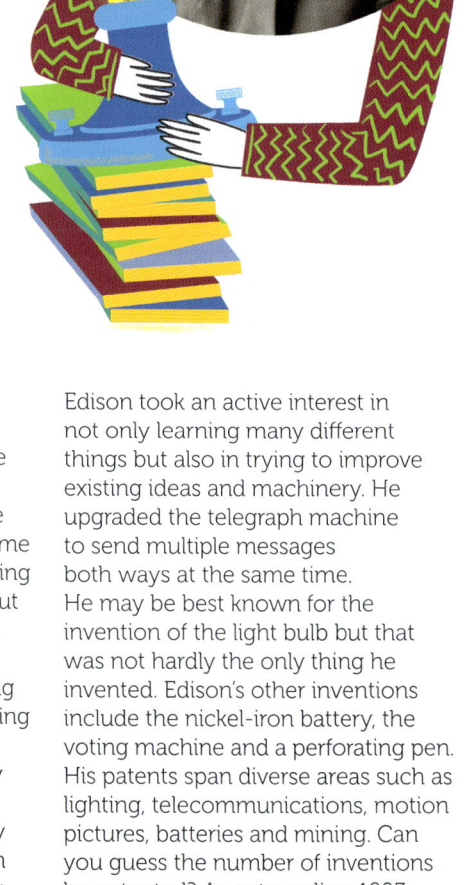

Thomas Alva Edison

The legendary light bulb moment! The light bulb became a reality in the 1870s through Thomas Alva Edison's persistent experimentation and efforts. The working bulb was the result of over 3000 different experiments that Edison tested out in his laboratory! The company he then formed—General Electric—is still one of the best-known global organizations associated with various energy, technology and engineering fields.

Edison received very little formal schooling. His teachers thought he was too distracted and not quite intelligent enough! He read a wide variety of books and studied at home with his mother. This homeschooling process served him well throughout his life. He set up his first chemical laboratory working on a train as a teenager. He had several interesting adventures including his lab catching fire one day! He, unfortunately, suffered a partial hearing loss early in his life, and yet he continued working unfazed, with his curiosity blazing. He first experimented with printing and became a telegrapher, and then a full-time inventor.

Edison took an active interest in not only learning many different things but also in trying to improve existing ideas and machinery. He upgraded the telegraph machine to send multiple messages both ways at the same time. He may be best known for the invention of the light bulb but that was not hardly the only thing he invented. Edison's other inventions include the nickel-iron battery, the voting machine and a perforating pen. His patents span diverse areas such as lighting, telecommunications, motion pictures, batteries and mining. Can you guess the number of inventions he patented? An astounding 1093 in the United States alone!

ELECTRIC CIRCUIT

Have you ever opened up a toy, a computer or a cell phone and found a green circuit board inside? Every device has a source of power and a source of electrical energy. It's very important that this energy gets to all parts of the device via the right route. Let's try building this route and see how it works.

MATERIALS

1 AA battery (1.5V)

Scissors

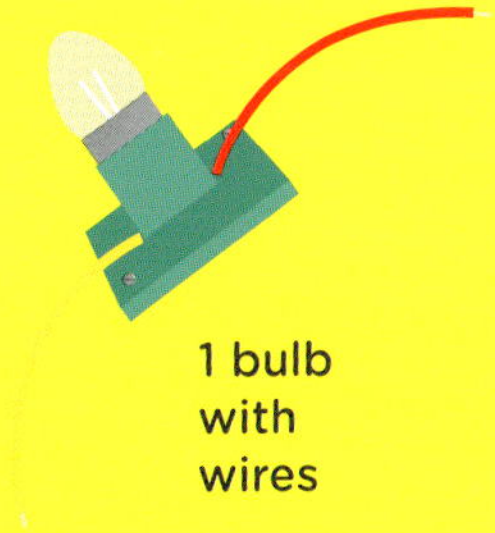

1 bulb with wires

A roll of conducting wire (copper or any other)

INSTRUCTIONS

1

Look out for the symbols '+' and '-' on the ends of the AA battery. The symbol '+' indicates the positive terminal and '-' indicates the negative terminal.

2

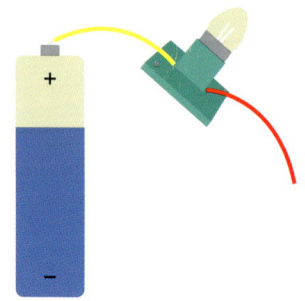

Connect any one wire of the bulb to the '+' terminal of the battery.

3

Connect the other wire of the bulb to the '-' terminal of the battery, thus completing the circuit as shown.

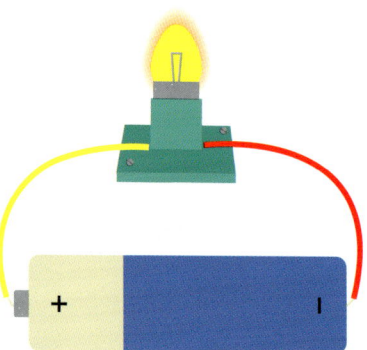

4

Watch the bulb glow as electricity flows from the battery to the bulb!

5

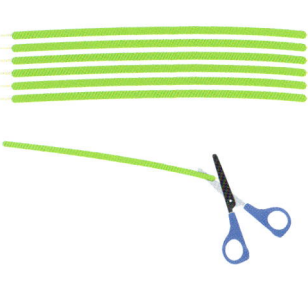

Cut twenty pieces of wire, each ten cm long, from the roll of conducting wire. Use the scissors to strip each of their ends.

6

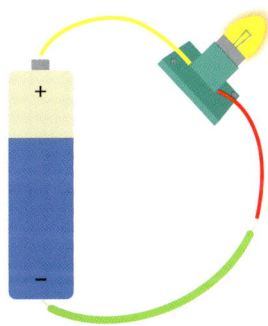

Connect the battery, bulb and one piece of wire to form a closed circuit as shown. Note the brightness of the bulb.

7

Take all the wires and twist their stripped ends together. Connect the battery and bulb to this to form a closed circuit as shown. Is the bulb brighter or dimmer?

8

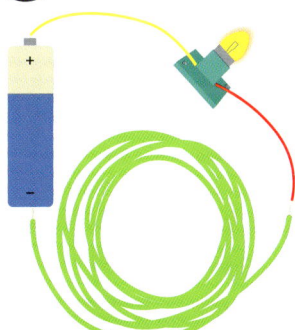

Use the battery, bulb and the remaining roll of wire (with stripped ends) to form a closed circuit as shown. Is the bulb brighter or dimmer?

DID YOU KNOW ?

a circuit needs to be circular to work. The path for the flow of electrons has to start at the power source and end there without any break or leakage in between.

Its important to note that some amount of electricity 'gets lost' when it travels through wires. Today's engineers are working on developing better wire materials so minimum electricity gets lost when it travels through them.

An electric circuit is a path made for electricity to flow through. Electricity consists of a flow of tiny charged balls, known as electrons. A battery or any other power source provides the pushing force that makes the electrons move. This pushing force is known as voltage and is represented by the symbol 'V'. When electrons get to a device like a light bulb or a laptop, they give it the power to work. The word circuit sounds like circle and

In the previous activity, the bulb is brightest when you connect it directly to the battery case and dimmest when you use the entire roll of wire in between. The more wire that gets used, the more electricity that is lost!

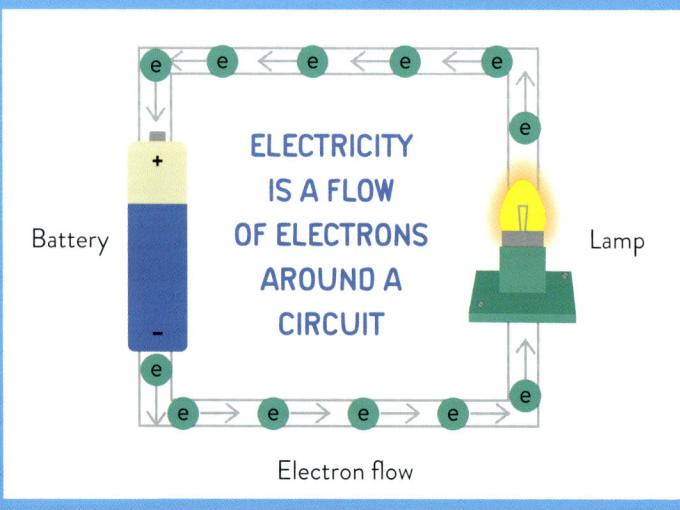

Battery

ELECTRICITY
IS A FLOW
OF ELECTRONS
AROUND A
CIRCUIT

Lamp

Electron flow

GREEN CIRCUIT BOARD

The green circuit board inside toys and computers is a board on which several electronic components are mounted. There is an intricate pathway that connects these components, allowing the electricity to flow from one component to another. But always remember, the electricity starts and ends at the terminals of the power source.

CONDUCTIVE EXPRESSWAY

Has anyone ever told you not to put your finger into an electrical socket? Or have you been warned not to fly kites near electric power lines? Do you know why you're not allowed to do this? It's because electricity can easily flow through certain kinds of materials and give you an electric shock! Let's understand what these safe (insulator) and unsafe (conductor) materials are.

MATERIALS

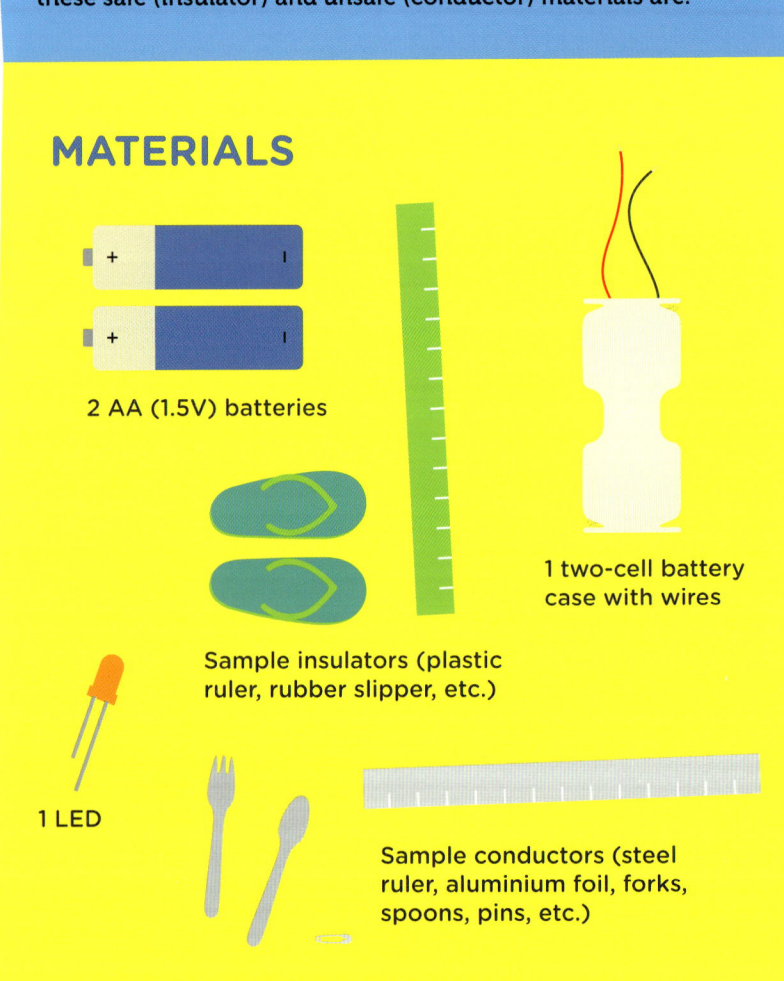

2 AA (1.5V) batteries

1 two-cell battery case with wires

Sample insulators (plastic ruler, rubber slipper, etc.)

1 LED

Sample conductors (steel ruler, aluminium foil, forks, spoons, pins, etc.)

INSTRUCTIONS

1

Insert the batteries into the battery case. To prevent a short circuit, ensure that the positive and negative wires of the battery case don't touch.

2

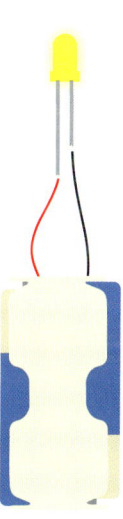

Connect the longer lead of the LED to the '+' (red) wire of the battery case and the shorter lead to the '-' (black) wire of the battery case as shown. Watch the LED light up.

3

Disconnect the shorter lead of the LED and the '-' (black) wire of the battery case. Leave the longer lead of the LED and the '+' (red) wire of the battery case connected as shown.

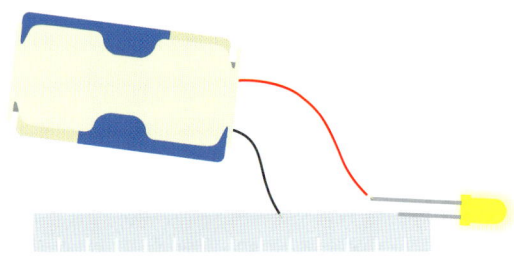

4

Place a conductor, such as a steel ruler, on a table. Connect the shorter lead of the LED to one end of the ruler.

5

Connect the '–' (black) wire of the battery case to the other end of the ruler. Watch the LED glow as the current passes through the ruler! .

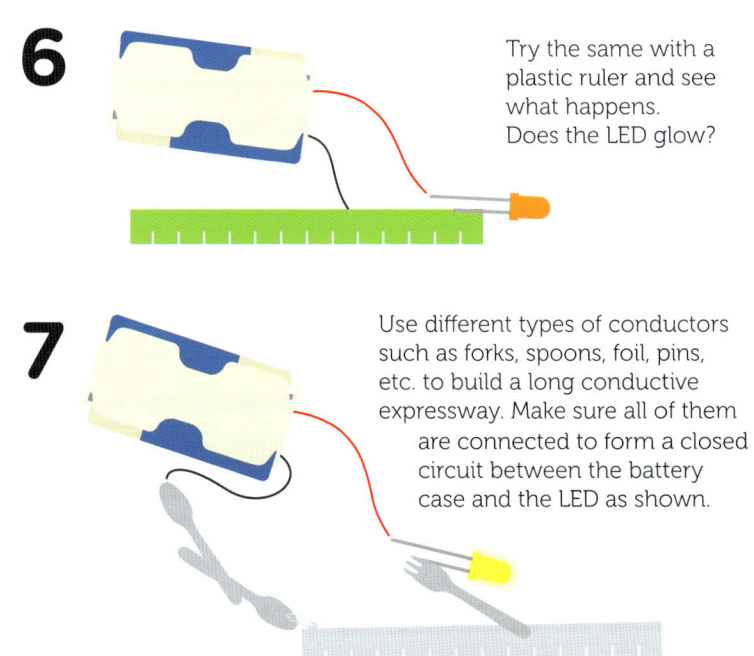

6

Try the same with a plastic ruler and see what happens.
Does the LED glow?

7

Use different types of conductors such as forks, spoons, foil, pins, etc. to build a long conductive expressway. Make sure all of them are connected to form a closed circuit between the battery case and the LED as shown.

DID YOU KNOW?

Conductors are materials through which electricity can flow through easily. They make organized use of electricity and electrical circuits possible. Some examples are metals, water, people, animals and trees.

Electricity always takes the shortest path to the ground. Your body consists of nearly sixty per cent water and that makes you a good conductor of electricity.

If an electric transmission power line has fallen on a tree and you

Electrocution

touch the tree, you become the path or conductor to the ground and can get electrocuted!

Insulators are materials that are the exact opposites of conductors. They prevent the flow of electricity. Some examples are glass, plastic and rubber.

Insulators are important to keep us safe from electricity. The wire that carries electricity to your computer or television is covered with a rubber-like material that protects you from getting electrocuted.

Some materials have the characteristics of both conductors and insulators. These materials

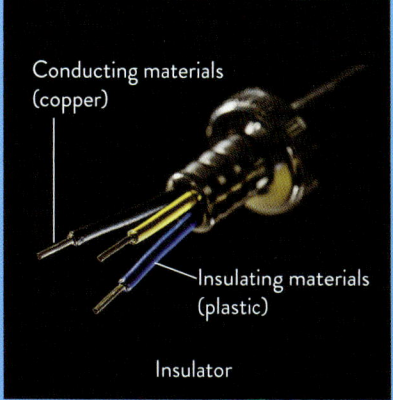

Conducting materials (copper)

Insulating materials (plastic)

Insulator

are called semiconductors. They allow electricity to flow through them under certain circumstances. Semiconductor materials have revolutionized the world of electronics and consequently our daily lives, which depend heavily on electronic gadgets. Silicon is the most commonly used semiconductor in electronics today.

The LED that you used in the above activity is a type of semiconductor. LEDs are versatile and are used in everything from TVs to traffic lights!

TRAFFIC LIGHTS WITH LED

BRAIN STORM

- Use the conductivity tester that you made in the activity to find ten conductors and ten insulators in your school or at home. Remember, a conductor will make your LED glow and an insulator will not!

- What do you think is the difference between an LED and a bulb? Experiment with a bulb, an LED and a battery case and list out three differences between an LED and a bulb. (Hint—try interchanging the connections of the LED/bulb with the battery case and see if it still works.)

TRIVIA

- LED bulbs can last at least twenty times longer than traditional bulbs. A good quality LED bulb can run constantly for over two years before it burns out!

- Silver and gold are among the best conductors of electricity. Gold is even used inside all our smart phones, laptops and computers!

SWITCH CIRCUIT

Flick it on and flick it off! Isn't it almost magical how you can control any electrical appliance with the turn of a switch? Let's find out how a switch works and what it is made of!

MATERIALS

2 AA (1.5V) batteries

1 LED

Insulation tape

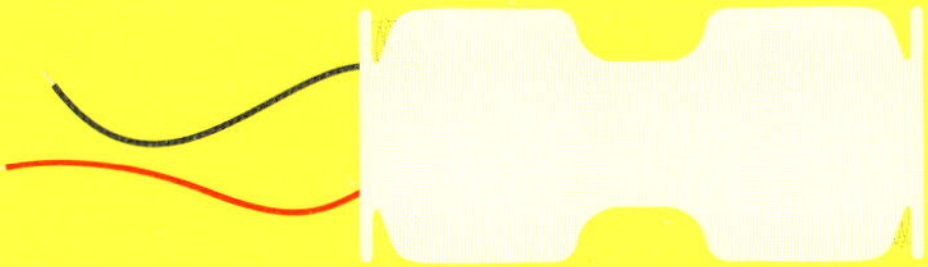

1 two-cell battery case with wires

Scissors

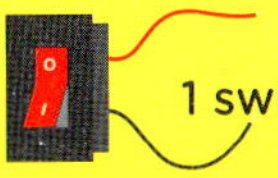

1 switch with wires

INSTRUCTIONS

1

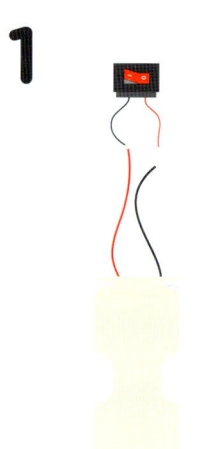

Connect any one wire of the switch to the '+' (red) wire of the battery case.

2

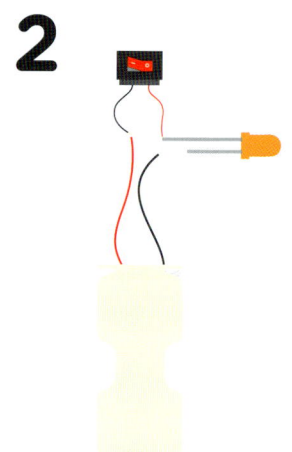

Connect the longer lead of the LED to the other wire of the switch.

3

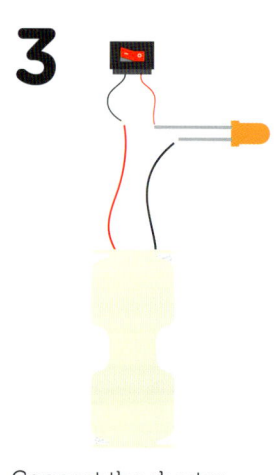

Connect the shorter lead of the LED to the '–' (black) wire of the battery case to complete the circuit as shown.

4

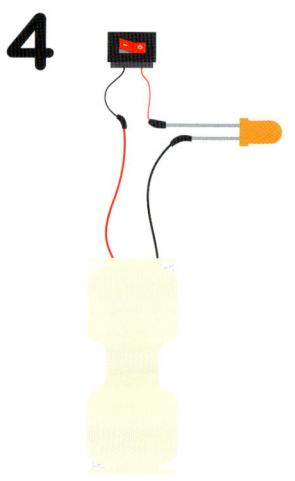

Put insulation tape over each connection individually.

5

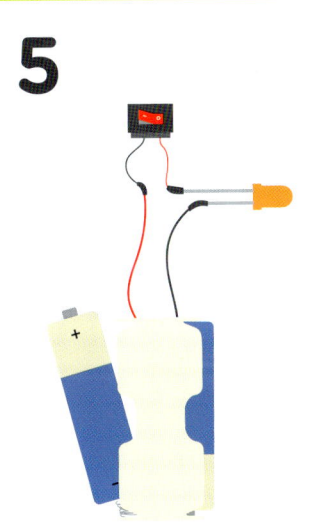

Insert the batteries into the battery case.

6

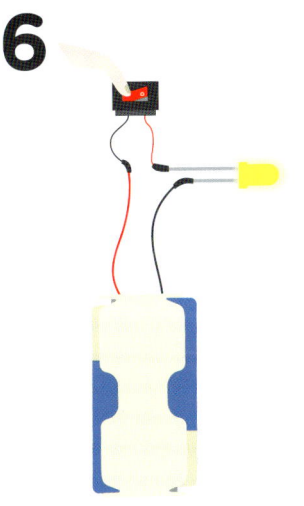

Operate the switch to turn the LED on and off.

7

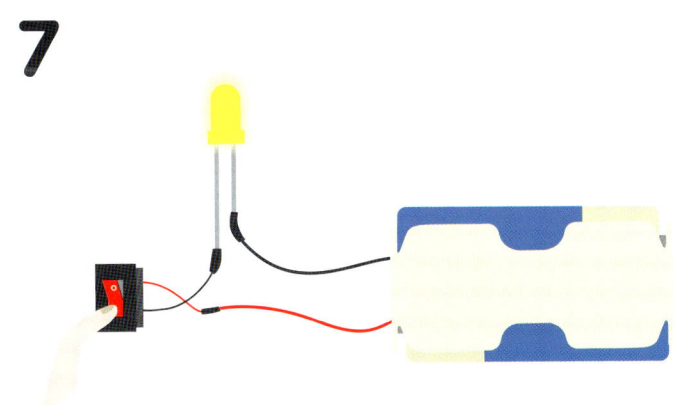

Rebuild the circuit by interchanging the connections of the switch as shown. Does the LED still light up? The LED will still light up as the switch used here does not have a '+' and a '-' terminal.

DID YOU KNOW?

Switches come in different types, sizes and have different uses. Understanding some of these types will help you choose the right switch for your invention.

Single Pole Single Throw (SPST): This is the switch you have used in the activity above and is the most common type of switch with two leads. Flipping the switch opens or closes the circuit by disconnecting or connecting the leads. These switches are used in table lamps, torches and household lighting.

Single Pole Dual Throw (SPDT): This switch has three leads and is used to control two devices. It does not have an off position and is known as a toggle switch. The centre lead can connect to either the left or the right lead depending on how the switch is used. This switch can be used to

A switch is a device which can be used to make or break a circuit. It acts like a bridge in the circuit. It has two metal contacts that touch to complete (make) a circuit, and separate to open (break) the circuit. When the switch is closed, it allows the flow of electricity. When the switch is open, it breaks the flow of electricity.

OFF OFF

ON

Switch

PUSH BUTTON SWITCHES
ON A KEYBOARD

BRAIN
STORM

- Use the battery case,
  batteries, switch
  and LED to:

  1. Design and build your
     very own portable
     torch (look at the
     bottle torch activity in
     the Design chapter).

  2. Design and build
     a table lamp.

TRIVIA

control a single light bulb from two different places as well to toggle between high beam and low beam in car headlights.

Push button switches: These switches are similar to SPST switches and have two leads. They are like buttons and are normally open. When the button is pressed, the circuit closes and the device comes on. Button switches can also be momentary which means that the switch will spring back to its rest position when it is not being pressed. Momentary button switches are used in keyboards, walkie-talkies and mobile phone keypads.

- A pressure switch is a type of switch that can be used to make a doorbell ring when someone steps on the doormat!

- Reed switches are switches that open or close a circuit when a magnetic field is present. These switches are used in door and window alarms to sense whether they are open!

HANDY FAN

What helps human beings move? Muscles, right? Well, machines need their own muscles too to help them move and these are known as motors. Motors are present in all things that move—fans, clocks, toy cars, gaming console controllers and even robots!

MATERIALS

1 twelve-inch plastic ruler

2 AA (1.5V) batteries

1 toy motor with wires

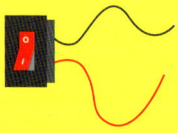

1 switch with long wires

1 toy propeller

Double-sided tape

1 two-cell battery case with wires

Insulation tape

INSTRUCTIONS

1

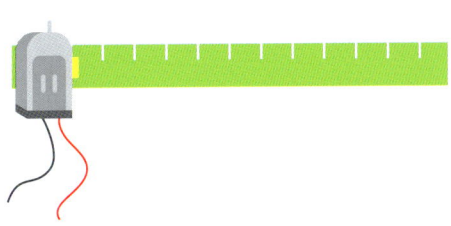

Use the double-sided tape to stick the toy motor to one end of the ruler.

2

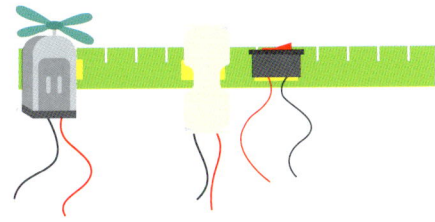

Stick the battery case and the switch on to the middle of the ruler as shown. Fix the propeller onto the toy motor shaft.

3

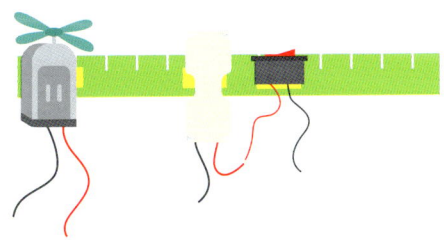

Connect any one wire of the switch to the '+' (red) wire of the battery case.

4

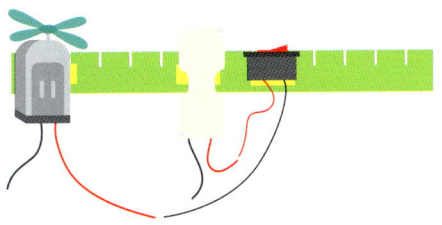

Connect the other wire of the switch to any one wire of the toy motor.

5

Complete the circuit by connecting the '-' (black) wire of the battery case to the other wire of the toy motor as shown.

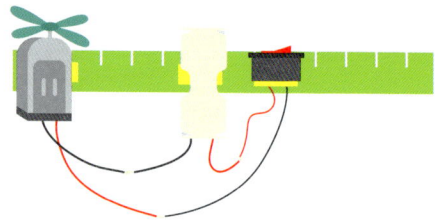

6

Put insulation tape over each connection individually. Tape all hanging wires together to prevent them from obstructing the movement of your fan.

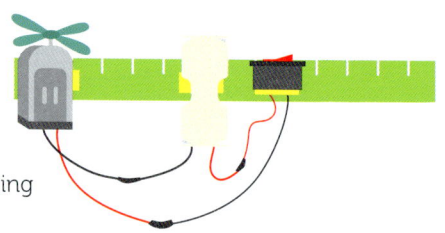

7

Insert the batteries into the battery case. Your handy fan is ready! Flick the switch on and off to see it in action.

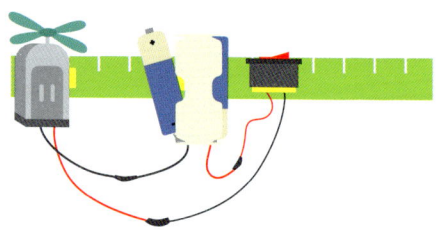

8

If you don't feel the gush of air from the propeller, try interchanging the connections between the battery case and the motor.

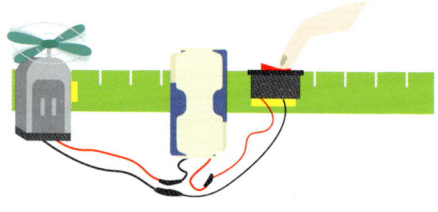

DID YOU KNOW ?

it becomes an electromagnet and develops a north and south pole. The permanent magnets that surround the coil attract and repel this electromagnet causing the motor to rotate.

If you want your invention to move, you will need to use a motor. Whether to rotate a platform, swing a door, or lift a weight, a motor can be the driving force to operate the mechanism.

A motor is a device that converts electrical energy to mechanical energy. It has revolutionized the fields of engineering and technology since the invention of electricity.

The motor works because of magnets and magnetism. It consists of a metal body and a cylindrical shaft. A copper coil is placed between two permanent magnets inside the motor. When electricity flows through this coil,

Motors are current-heavy devices, unlike LEDs, and you need to choose the right type of motor for the job. Using the wrong motor can result in underperformance and in the worst case, the invention failing completely!

This table introduces you to some types of motors and their applications. You should now be able to choose the right motor for any invention.

Name of Motor	Brief Description	Applications	
DC (direct current) Motor	Most common type of battery-operated motor. Small and doesn't require complicated control.	CD-ROM drives, printers, toy cars, CPU fans	
AC (alternating current) Motor	Cannot be powered by batteries. Needs special connections and spins at a constant speed.	Heavy industries that require continuous operation, refrigerator compressors, electric model plane engines	

Servo Motor	Has built-in gears to increase torque. Has a built-in controller. Very accurate in its movement.	Control the movement of model airplanes, moving robotic limbs	
Stepper Motor	Offers the greatest precision. Very slow and bulky.	Plotters, card readers, photocopy machines	

BRAIN STORM

- Spot three devices in your house or school that use motors. Use the motor table as a guide and figure out which type of motor each device uses.

- Use a copper wire, battery and magnets to try and create your own working motor.

TRIVIA

- Motors are used to propel electric cars. The rechargeable batteries of the car power these motors.

- Robotics makes great use of motors because they help robots move in multiple ways like throwing a ball, holding a can or saluting you!

TOUCH LIGHT

Your brain is made up of billions of cells called neurons, which are tiny switches that let you think and remember things. Computers and electronic gadgets contain billions of mini-brain cells, too. They're called transistors and they're semiconductors made from silicon. Let's try out a fun activity using a transistor!

MATERIALS

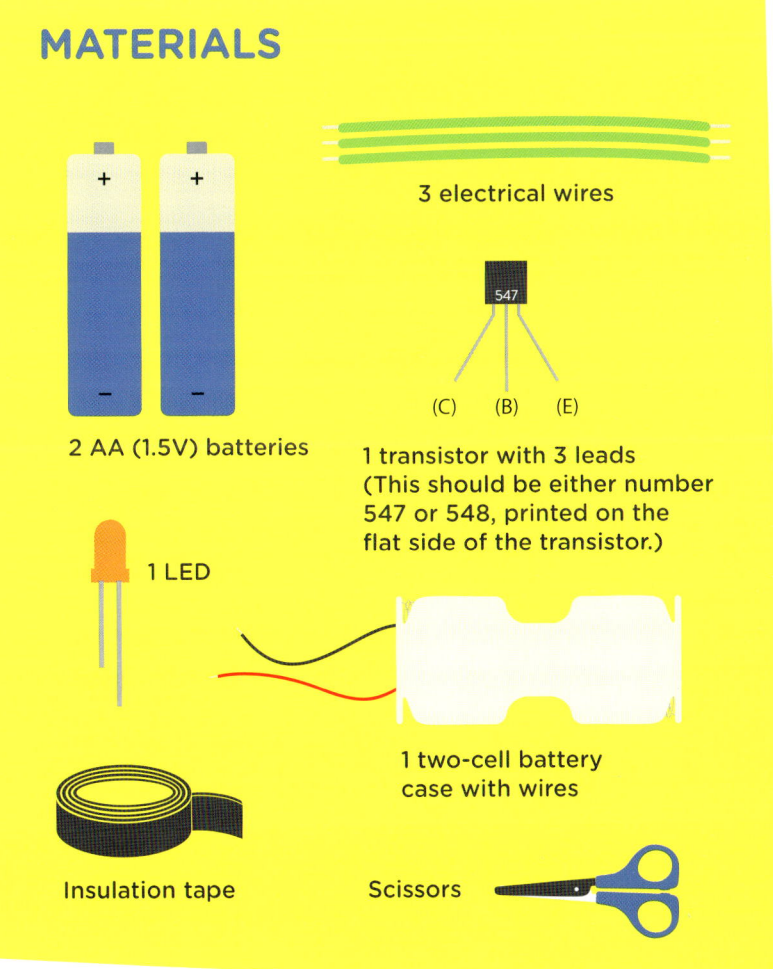

3 electrical wires

(C) (B) (E)

2 AA (1.5V) batteries

1 transistor with 3 leads
(This should be either number 547 or 548, printed on the flat side of the transistor.)

1 LED

1 two-cell battery case with wires

Insulation tape

Scissors

INSTRUCTIONS

1

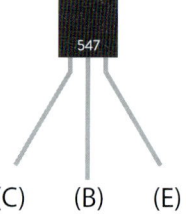

(C)　　(B)　　(E)

Hold the transistor upright so that the flat side is facing you as shown. The left lead is called the Collector (C), the middle lead is called the Base (B) and the right lead is called the Emitter (E).

2

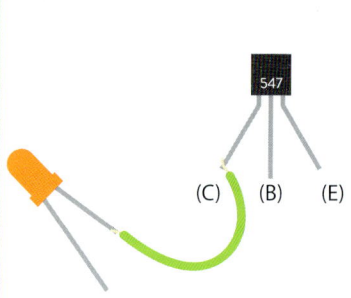

(C)　　(B)　　(E)

Use one electrical wire to connect the shorter lead of the LED to the C lead of the transistor as shown.

3

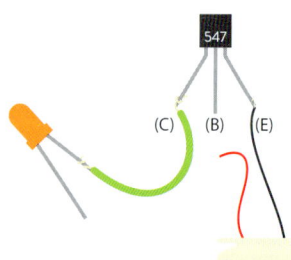

(C)　(B)　(E)

Connect the '–' (black) wire of the battery case to the E lead of the transistor as shown.

4

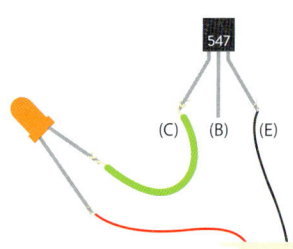

(C)　(B)　(E)

Connect the '+' (red) wire of the battery case to the longer lead of the LED as shown.

5

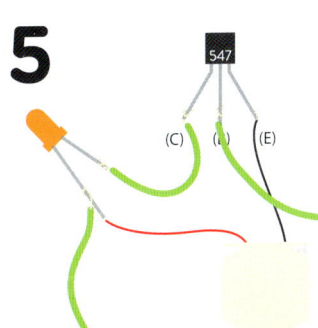

Using the two other electrical wires, connect one wire to the B lead of the transistor and the other wire to the longer lead of the LED as shown. Do not connect anything to the other ends of these wires.

6

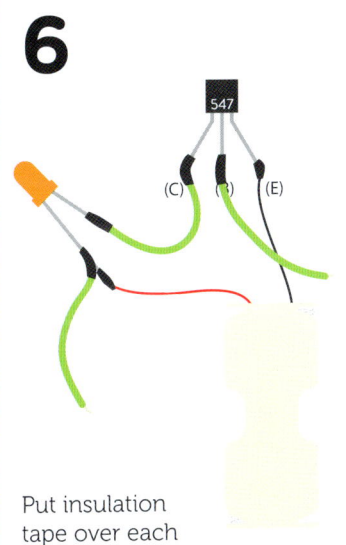

Put insulation tape over each connection individually.

7

Insert the batteries into the battery case.

8

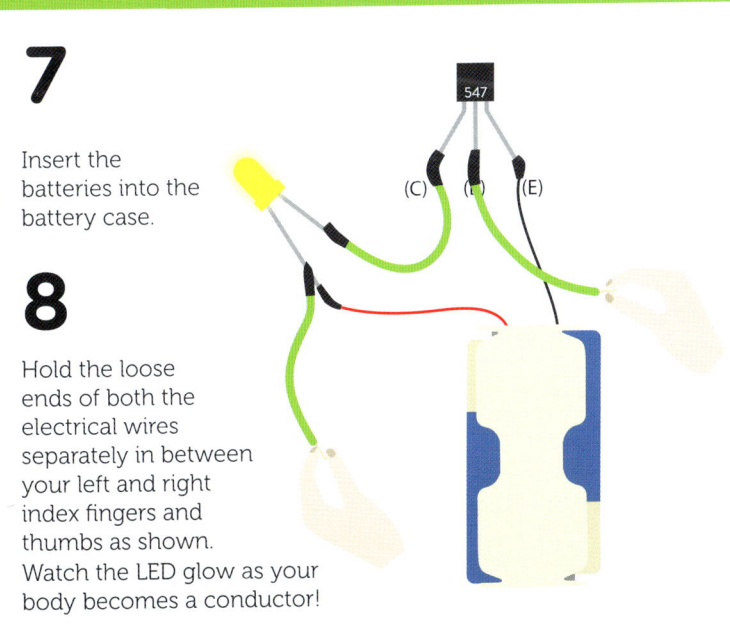

Hold the loose ends of both the electrical wires separately in between your left and right index fingers and thumbs as shown. Watch the LED glow as your body becomes a conductor!

DID YOU KNOW?

The tiny yet mighty transistor is central to all electronic circuitry today. It was invented in 1947 and has transformed the world of electronics. None of our favourite electronic devices—touchscreen phones, laptops or tablets—would exist without transistors.

Transistors are electronic marvels that let you control the flow of electricity by controlling the movement of electrons. A transistor can work as an amplifier or as a sensitive switch. As an amplifier, it works like a current booster—taking a tiny input current and producing a bigger output current. The use of transistors in hearing aids and radios is an example of this application.

As a sensitive switch, it triggers a current flow on sensing a small current. The use of transistors in computers and memory chips is an example of this application.

Transistors are manufactured in different shapes but the common feature is their three leads:

Base: Activates the transistor
Collector: Positive lead
Emitter: Negative lead

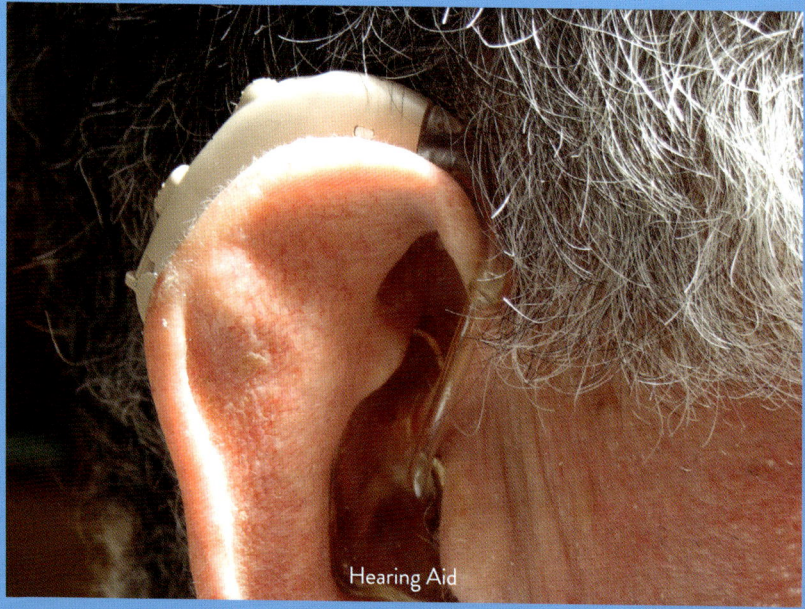

Hearing Aid

RADIO

Do you remember that the human body is a good conductor of electricity? In our activity here, when we touch the base of the transistor and the positive wire of the battery case, current flows from the battery case through our body to the base! This activates the transistor and a path for the electricity is created from the battery case via the LED.

When a current flows through the base of the transistor, it switches on the transistor causing the collector and emitter to connect internally.

TRIVIA

BRAIN STORM

- For a fun experience, form a human chain holding hands with your friends and watch the LED glow!

- Try the human chain activity wearing gloves.

- Gordon Moore, co-founder of Intel, predicted that the number of transistors on a computer chip would double about every two years. This is known as Moore's Law. This has allowed computing devices to get smaller and smaller!

- The first Intel computer chip had 2300 transistors, while the latest one consists of 820 million!

THE FUTURE WORLD OF ELECTRICITY

Imagine a world where all your electronic gadgets could chat amongst themselves. So, for example, your alarm clock would tell the geyser to switch on and the geyser, in turn, would inform the toaster, 'Bath done, pop out the toast!' And when you step out of your house, the gate would lock your door and ask all the gadgets to go to sleep until you return in the evening!

Welcome to the world of smart gadgets and networks!

INTELLIGENT SYSTEMS

The Internet of things is a network of electronic devices that can exchange information amongst one another. This is an exciting new technological development. Smart electronics has made our environment more interactive, more intelligent and has also optimized the use of electricity.

For example, temperature, motion and light sensors integrated into our home electric systems ensure that our homes are warm when we arrive, water is hot when required and the lights and heating are turned off when we leave.

WIRELESS ELECTRICITY

Tired of wires and tangles everywhere? The future will be wireless—powered by witricity or wireless electricity. Normally, electricity is carried from the point of generation to the point of usage through wires. Remember the charged balls moving through wires at great speeds? Wireless electricity travels through mutual induction between magnetic

fields; it requires no wires! In the future, most devices would be able to use witricity to charge themselves from an electric source nearby! .

SMART E-WARDROBE

Can you imagine the curtains of your living room and bedroom turning into a TV? Imagine your tracksuit being able to store all your favourite music and playing it when you touch your sleeve! How would a curtain, a tracksuit or a musical keyboard jacket get the electricity required to work? They could either charge wirelessly or generate their own electricity using the movements of the user or even have a string battery sewn into the hem. Sounds like a science fiction story? Well, it could soon come true!

The development of digital yarn, e-textiles and wearable electronics will soon bring out smart clothing that can double up as communication devices, health monitors, navigation systems, data storage and what not. The possibilities are exciting!

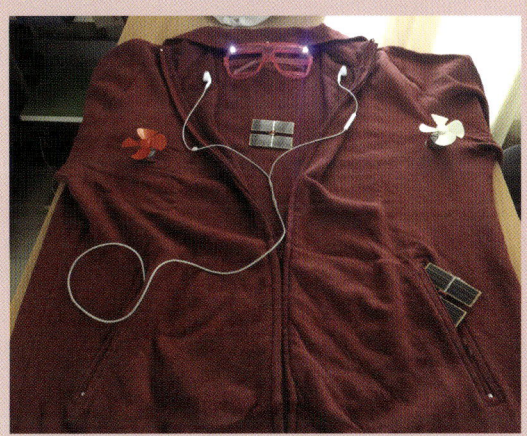

SMART GRIDS

Electricity generated in power stations travels thousands of miles to reach our homes through a network of cables, transformers and wires. The transmission and distribution grid plays an important role to ensure that the power supply is at a steady voltage

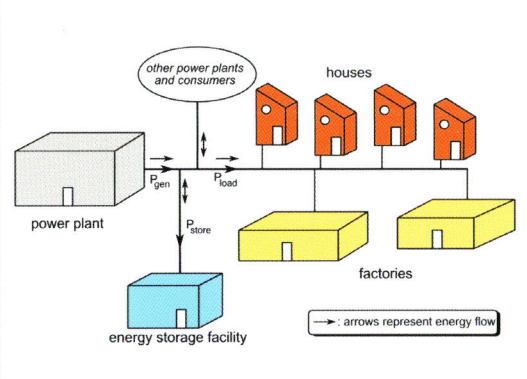

and uninterrupted. A smart grid continuously takes input from household meters to understand consumption patterns better. This data helps the grid decide where and how to direct the electricity supply. It also helps electricity companies set different unit rates for the electricity depending on the number of units consumed.

DESIGN THE FUTURE

Now that we know a little more about how we can generate and control electricity, how about designing your own electronic gadget?

BRAINSTORM
Think about integrating your clothing with electronics. Would you like to add LEDs or a cooling fan to your clothes? How about adding a mobile charging slot? What would you put to power all these up? Design and draw out your version of a futuristic jacket!

Machines

'It is only when they go wrong that machines remind you how powerful they are.'
CLIVE JAMES

INTRODUCTION

Machines are everywhere. The toaster that pops out a perfect—crisp and evenly browned—toast for you every morning is a machine. The bus that takes you to your school is a machine. Even that simple slide and merry-go-round in the playground are machines! The bicycle you love to ride in the evenings is a machine and so is your favourite toy car. Some are big, some are small, some look simple and some seem really complicated!

So what exactly are machines?

You probably would have heard of simple machines such as pulleys, inclined planes, wedges, screws, wheels and axles. Machines are things that help us reduce our effort when we do some work. Machines generally have parts that move. They utilize forces such as push and pull to make doing our work easier. Tools and machines have been an important part of human evolution. It was the invention of the wheel that made it possible to build carts, allowing people to travel over great distances, thus taking human civilization to new, unexplored places. The invention of the wedge simplified cutting wood and other materials to make useful objects, while the inclined plane helped transport things up and down to build taller structures.

The Industrial Revolution was essentially an age of machines.

It started around 1760 and transitioned old-fashioned production processes to new and efficient machine-driven processes. Steam engines, industrial machines, trains, ships, automobiles and many more complex machines were engineered. They changed the way human beings led their lives.

Industrial machines made large-scale production possible. People were able to manufacture things easily in huge numbers and at a lower cost. All kinds of factories were set up. New transportation systems and engines made it easy to travel around the world, making business and communication global in nature.

The progress of mankind is closely interwoven with the evolution of machines, and will continue to be so. It is important for us to learn how these mechanisms work, so we can better understand how the modern world around us works. As an inventor you can use simple machines in many efficient ways in order to make your inventions work better and faster.

Industrial Revolution

THE MECHANICAL INVENTOR

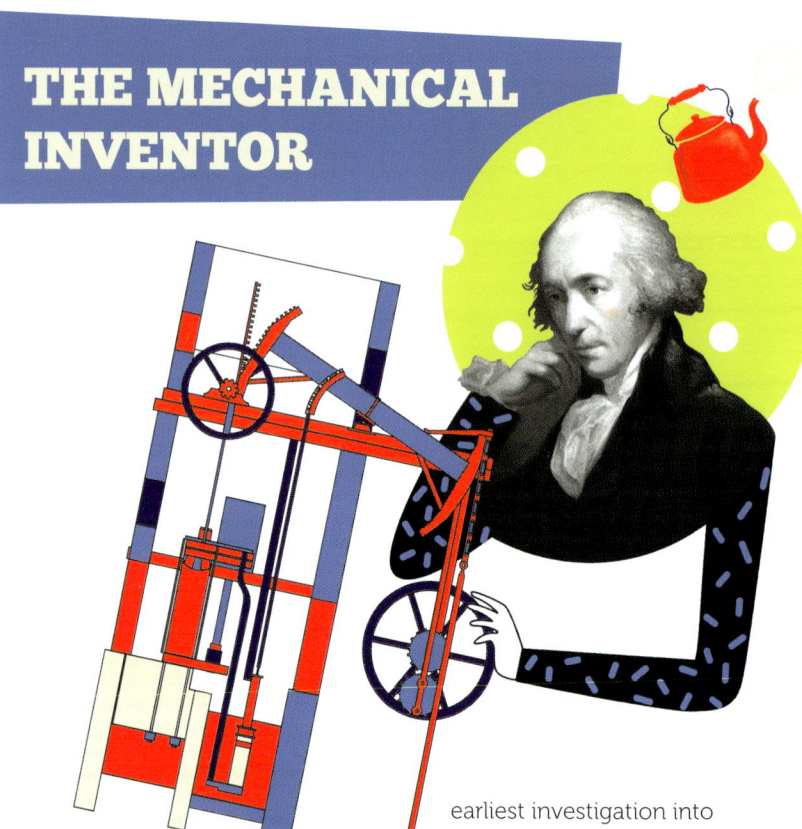

James Watt

James Watt was the inventor of the steam machine that made large-scale industrialization possible. Have you heard the stories of his childhood days? He was home-schooled because his poor health did not let him attend regular school. At home, he learnt the basics of engineering and tooling from his father's carpentry tools. At the age of six, James Watt occupied himself by solving geometrical problems, and by experimenting with his mother's tea kettle—his earliest investigation into the nature of steam!

At eighteen, he started his apprenticeship and learnt all about mechanical instruments. He spent his working hours building and repairing various mechanical gadgets such as mathematical, nautical and musical instruments. It was while he was repairing a model of the Newcomen's Engine that he started his own study of steam engines.

Tinkering with tools and instruments, opening things up and trying to put them back together can create an inventive mind just like that of James Watt! Let's see how this can be done by building and engineering some really cool machines!

DOODLE BOT

What happens when your mobile phone rings in silent mode? It vibrates, of course! Vibration is fast becoming a way by which gadgets send information to humans. Let's see how we can use vibration to create a doodle bot that vibrates around and makes artistic doodles on your paper canvas!

MATERIALS

Scissors

One 9 Volt battery

1 medium-sized paper cup

1 500-ml bottle cap

4 small sketch pens

1 toy motor with wires

Insulation tape

Double-sided tape

One 9 Volt battery snap with wires

1 switch with wires

Fevicol

INSTRUCTIONS

1

Stick the sketch pens around the outside of the paper cup using the double-sided tape as shown.

2

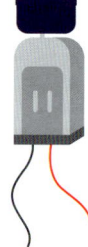

Insert the shaft of the motor on to one side of the bottle cap as shown.

3

Turn the cup over. Use double-sided tape to stick the battery on to the base of the cup. Ensure the cup is balanced properly.

4

Use double-sided tape and stick the motor and switch on top of the battery as shown.

5

Connect any one wire of the switch to the '+' (red) wire of the battery snap. Connect the other wire of the switch to any wire of the motor.

6

Connect the '-' (black) wire of the battery snap and the unconnected wire of the motor to complete the circuit.

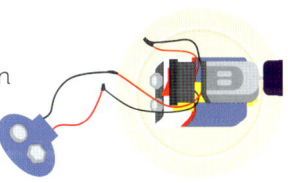

7

Put insulation tape over each connection individually. Tape all hanging wires together in a neat bunch so they don't obstruct the movement of your bot.

8

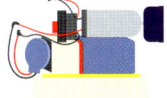

Fix the battery snap on to the battery.

9

Place your doodle bot on a blank paper, switch it on and watch it doodle!

DID YOU KNOW ?

This cool new technology is known as haptics.

The word haptic originated from the Greek word 'haptikos' which means pertaining to the sense of touch. Vibration is used as a type of haptic technology in a number of gadgets today. Some examples include mobile phones and video game controllers. These devices have special tiny vibrating motors with unbalanced weights. The

Our artistic bot uses the concept of vibration to work. How do we create this vibrating motion? The motor has an off-centre unbalanced weight attached to it. In the previous activity, the bottle cap is used to create an imbalance of weight which makes the bot vibrate when the motor spins. Vibration can provide feedback to human by taking advantage of the humans' sense of touch.

rotation of these motors during the working of the device causes the vibrating alert in them.

This technology can be of more use than just serving as an alert! Picture this—you're playing 'Angry Birds' on your

Vibration Motor Inside a Cell Phone

HOLOGRAM

BRAIN STORM

- Repeat the activity by fixing the shaft of the motor at different points on the bottle cap (centre, left, right, etc.). Does your bot vibrate differently?

TRIVIA

- A hologram is a 3D image that is projected using light. Haptic holograms can use vibration and actually interact with humans!

- Haptic holograms allow for mutual touch. People will be able to reach out and physically touch a hologram. What's more, they'll feel a sensation in return, such as their hand being squeezed by the hologram!

tablet and when you stretch the string, you could actually feel the tension or tightness of the string. This could possible through a special gear that you are wearing! Wouldn't that be awesome? The possibilities can be as crazy as the game developer's imagination! Ambient vibration is present all around us in sounds and in surfaces such as floors, rail tracks, speed breakers and ocean waves. These vibrations can also be used as a source of energy. In the future, the energy harvested from the vibration inside a machine may be able to power up the machine!

HYDRAULIC LIFT

Did you ever think that you could use air, water or oil to help your machine do more work? Ever wondered how cranes, forklifts and JCBs are able to lift objects that are super heavy? Welcome to the world of hydraulics and pneumatics!

MATERIALS

2 ten-ml syringes
(without needles)

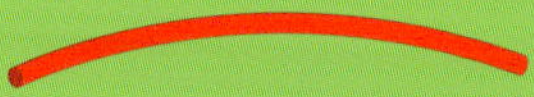

1 twelve-inch piece of plastic tubing that fits snugly on to the syringe hose

1 open shoe box

An empty matchbox

Double-sided tape

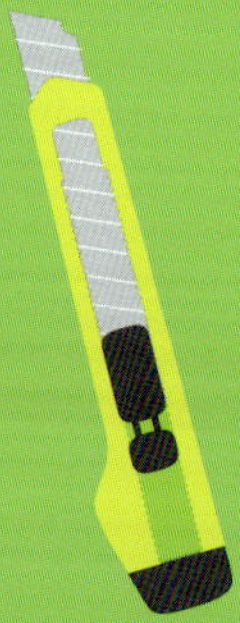

1 box cutter blade

INSTRUCTIONS

1

Place the shoebox
vertically on a table.

2

Hold the syringe with the
plunger on top. Stick the
syringe on the inside wall
of the shoebox, close to
the base, using the
double-sided tape as shown.

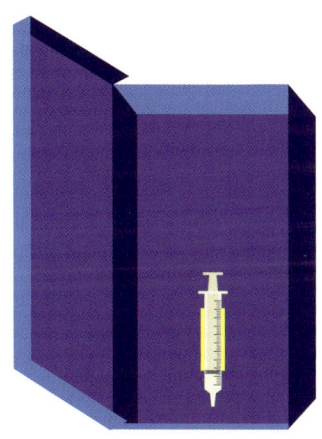

3

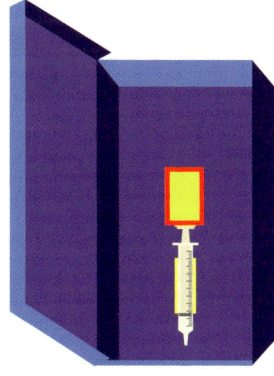

Stick the matchbox
vertically on top of the
syringe plunger using
double sided tape.

4

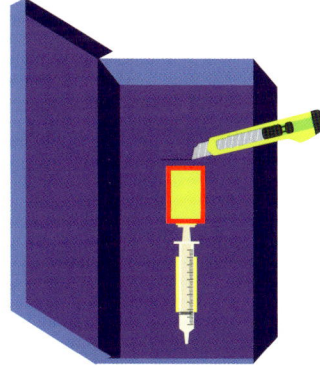

From the inside wall of the
shoebox, cut open a slit above
the level of the matchbox.
This is the upper floor.

5

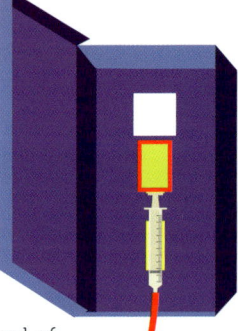

Fix one end of the plastic tubing on to the hose of the syringe inside the shoebox.

6

Take the other syringe and fill it with water.

7

Fix the other end of the plastic tubing on to the hose of the water-filled syringe.

8

Ensure that there are no air bubbles inside the syringes.

9

You can colour the shoebox to make it look like a building. You can also colour the matchbox and paste a human figure on it.

10

Gently push and pull the plunger of the syringe that is outside the shoebox and watch your matchbox lift moving up and down!

DID YOU KNOW ?

such as lifts, dump trucks, braking systems, cranes, car jacks and so on.

When designing a hydraulic system, you need to give some thought to what liquid to use as the hydraulic fluid. The more incompressible the liquid, the better the system works. There are other considerations, too, while deciding on the perfect hydraulic fluid. For instance, fluid for farm equipment should be natural oil so it does not harm the soil.

Hydraulics is an branch of science engineering. It focuses the use of fluids to mechanical tasks. Typically, the fluid in a hydraulic system incompressible liquid water or oil. A simple of a hydraulic system be two cylinders and connected via a pipe, the two syringes and you have just used.

Cylinders have a certain of incompressible liquid So what happens is that when you push the because the liquid be compressed, it flows into the other cylinder pushing the piston up. This is how the force that you apply on one part of the system gets transmitted to the other part.

Hydraulic systems use a combination of different sizes of cylinders and pistons to use less force to do more work. These are used in big machines

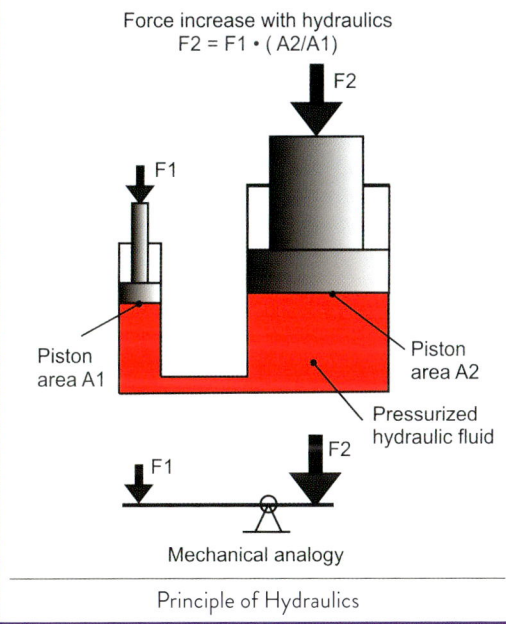

Force increase with hydraulics
$$F2 = F1 \cdot (A2/A1)$$

F2

F1

Piston area A1

Piston area A2

Pressurized hydraulic fluid

F1   F2

Mechanical analogy

Principle of Hydraulics

Pneumatics works in the same way as hydraulics. Hydraulics uses the pressure of the trapped liquid, whereas pneumatics makes use of trapped air inside cylinders. Air brakes on buses and trucks are examples of pneumatics.

Hydraulics and pneumatics are the mainstays of many heavy

Hydraulic Digger

machines. As an inventor, you can explore ways of using the tremendous power of air pressure and liquid pressure to make your inventions perform herculean tasks with a fingertip push!

BRAIN STORM

- In the above activity, replace the 10-ml syringe inside the shoebox with a 20-ml syringe and operate your lift. Do you notice any change in the force that is required to make your lift move?

- Remove the water from the syringes and try the activity by filling the syringes with oil and air respectively. Observe the movement of your lift. Do you notice any change?

TRIVIA

- Car brakes work because of hydraulics. When you put your foot on the brake pedal, a hydraulic fluid transmits that force to a disc that in turn stops the wheels.

HOVERCRAFT POLO

What role do you think friction plays in our daily lives? Is friction a good or a bad thing? Can you think of how friction helps us walk and helps cars brake? But is friction good for machines, especially the ones that have moving parts inside them? Let's find out!

MATERIALS

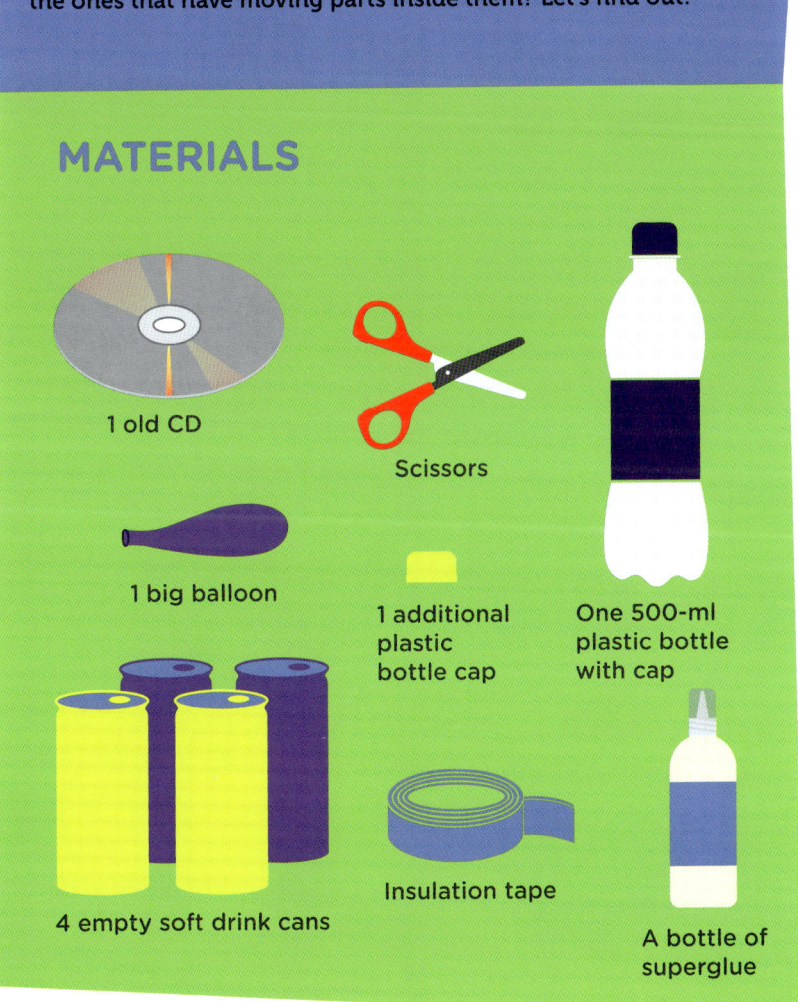

1 old CD

Scissors

1 big balloon

1 additional plastic bottle cap

One 500-ml plastic bottle with cap

4 empty soft drink cans

Insulation tape

A bottle of superglue

INSTRUCTIONS

1

Unscrew the cap of the plastic bottle and make a hole in the centre using the scissor as shown.

2

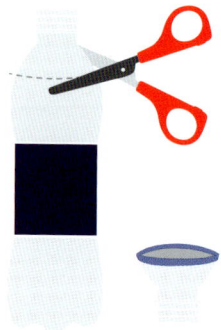

Cut out the neck of the plastic bottle and tape the cut edge with insulation tape as shown.

3

Fix the balloon on to the cut end of the bottle neck.

4

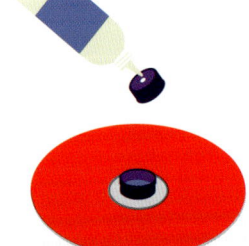

Place the CD on a table with the shiny side facing down. Take the bottle cap with the hole. Use superglue to stick its flat side on to the CD hole as shown.

5

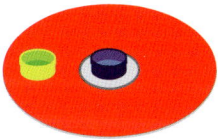

On the same side of the CD, stick the other bottle cap anywhere near the outer edge using superglue. This will help your hovercraft move straight.

6

Blow air into the balloon through the mouth of the cut bottle neck. Twist the balloon to ensure that no air escapes.

7

Screw in the bottle neck with the attached balloon to the central bottle cap on the CD as shown.

8

Place the soda cans as goalposts on opposite ends of the smooth surface. Place your CD hovercraft on a smooth surface such as a glass table. Let go of the balloon by allowing the air to escape. Push the CD slightly to start your game of hovercraft polo!

against the floor. Essentially your CD hovercraft travels on a cushion of air—like a flying carpet!

Most real-life hovercrafts use large fans which force air to move under the craft. A skirt made of rubber or fabric traps this air. Additional fans are attached to blow air towards the back of the hovercraft, causing it to move forward.

Try pushing a CD across the floor. It does not travel smoothly or too far because the surfaces of the CD and the floor rub against each other, creating friction. This friction hampers the movement of the CD.

But in our balloon hovercraft, when you release the air from the balloon, it gushes out and goes under the CD. This layer of air reduces the friction because it prevents the CD from rubbing

Because hovercrafts float on a pocket of air, they are able to travel over many different surfaces including water, snow and sand thus making them versatile machines!

Reducing friction is an important task in the process of machine design. Wherever there are moving parts inside the machinery, there will be some friction, which reduces the speed and efficiency of these machines.

Hovercraft

BALL BEARING

- Try the above activity with both a small and big balloon. Do you notice any difference in the movement of your hovercraft?

- Attach a small weight (a sharpener or an eraser) at different points of your hovercraft and try to control its direction of movement.

TRIVIA

It increases the consumption of energy and wear and tear of the moving parts. However, friction is not always bad. Some degree of friction is essential to help us do everyday tasks such as drive a car, pick up objects and even walk! In the absence of friction, everything would just slip and slide away. As an inventor, you need to remember this and design machines in a manner that optimizes the effect of friction. In most machines, you will find ball bearings, air cushions, oil and grease being used to reduce friction and its effects.

- During the 1950s, an Englishman named Christopher Cockerell developed and patented the first hovercraft.

- A hovercraft will move faster over ice than over land or water. Smoother the surface, lesser the friction!

BOTTLE BOAT

Have you ever travelled on a boat or a ship? Or used a knife to cut a fruit or vegetable in the kitchen? Wait! How in the world are boats and knives related? Let's find out.

MATERIALS

1 toy propeller

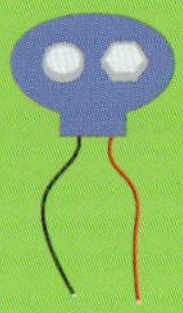

One 9 Volt battery snap with wires

Two 500-ml empty plastic bottles with caps

One 9 Volt battery

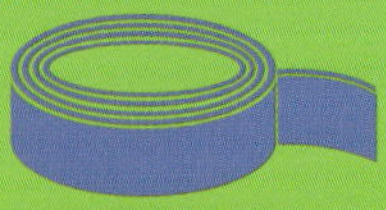

Insulation tape

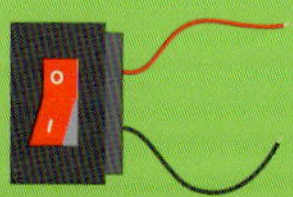

1 switch with wires

1 toy motor with wires

Double-sided tape

INSTRUCTIONS

1

Tape the bottles together using insulation tape. Make sure they are aligned as shown.

2

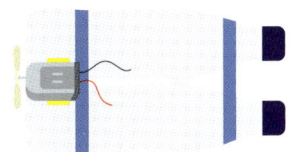

Fix the propeller on to the motor shaft. Use double-sided tape to stick the motor in between the rear ends of the bottles ensuring free movement of the propeller.

3

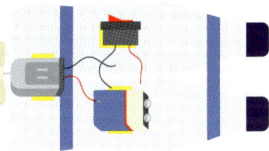

Stick the switch and battery on to the middle of the bottles using the double-sided tape as shown.

4

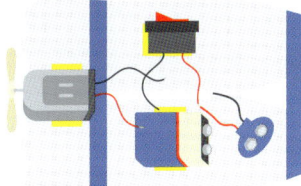

Connect any wire of the switch to the '+' (red) wire of the battery snap.

5

Connect the other wire of the switch to any wire of the motor.

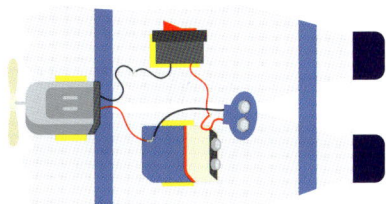

6

Connect the '–' (black) wire of the battery snap and the unconnected wire of the motor. This completes the circuit.

7

Put insulation tape over each connection individually. Tape all hanging wires as a bunch to prevent them from obstructing the movement of your boat.

8

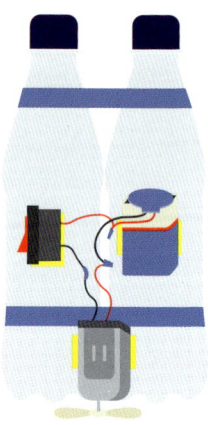

Affix the battery snap on to the battery.

9

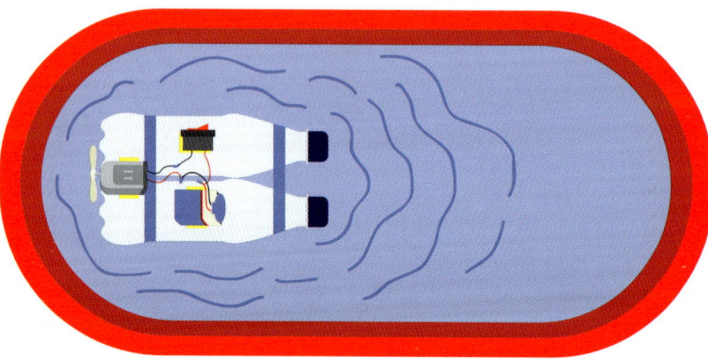

Place your bottle boat gently into a tub of water, switch on the motor and watch your boat sail away!

DID YOU KNOW ?

many different simple machines and the laws of physics to make it work. Boats normally have aerodynamic shapes, typically a tapering front end. This acts like a common simple machine known as a 'wedge'. A good example of a wedge is a kitchen knife. Just like a kitchen knife slices through a fruit or a vegetable, the front end of a boat cuts through water efficiently. In our model, air is propelling the boat forward. In the real world, a special type of boat, known as the sailboat, uses natural wind to propel itself. The direction of the sail can be changed to control the direction in which the boat moves. The device used to steer other boats, ships, submarines and aircraft is called a rudder. It is an interesting mechanism that uses a vertical plane to deflect the force of air and water to change the direction of movement.

Vehicles are easily some of the best-known and loved machines because they make our lives so much simpler. Starting from tricycles, scooters, cars, trucks, buses and trains to airplanes, all transport vehicles are machines that have changed the way we live.

Inventors of these machines spent years improving their designs, trying to make better vehicles. Boats have evolved over the centuries from being simple rafts to becoming huge ships and luxury liners. A boat is a complex machine that relies on

As an aspiring inventor, you might want to pay some attention to boat design and the material used for boat building. Good boat material

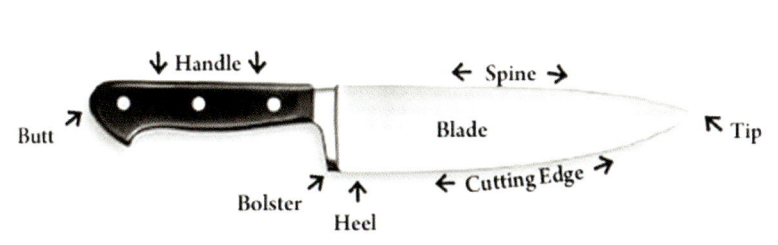

Simple Machine Wedge

needs to be lightweight, water-resistant, rust-proof, long-lasting and cost-effective. Apart from the material, the shape and design of the boat play an important role in its performance. Distributing the weight over a large area is another key component of boat design.

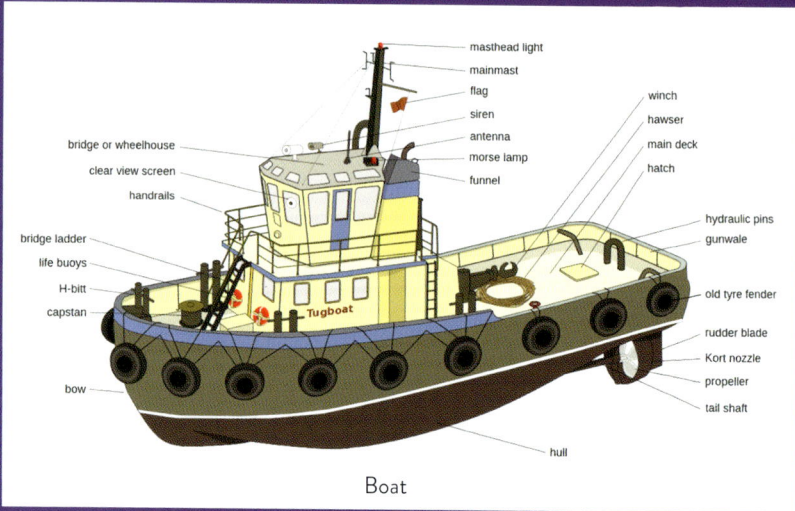

Boat

BRAIN STORM

- Attach a rudder to your boat and try to control its movement.

- Can you figure out a way to make your boat move backwards?

- Design a small house on your boat and build a futuristic floating house!

TRIVIA

- You probably use a wedge every day. A fork is considered a wedge. It is made up of four to five wedges together. It can be used to cut or slice food.

CATAPULT

Let's say you are sitting at home and are bored. Can you think of a cool target-hitting device to kill your boredom and your enemies? All hail the catapult! Catapults were invented as devices to hurl objects farther than any human could. They proved very effective as weapons on battlefields and have been used since ancient times all the way up to World War I!

MATERIALS

8 ice-cream sticks

5 medium-sized rubber bands

1 hard, strong plastic spoon (the length must be lesser than that of the ice-cream sticks)

Ammunition (nuts, ball bearings, small stones, paper balls, etc.)

1 target board

INSTRUCTIONS

1

Stack five ice-cream sticks together and put two rubber bands around them, one on each end to hold the sticks tightly together.

2

Stack the remaining three sticks and put a rubber band over one end.

3

Insert the centre of the five-stick stack through the three-stick stack in such a way that there is one stick on top and two sticks below as shown.

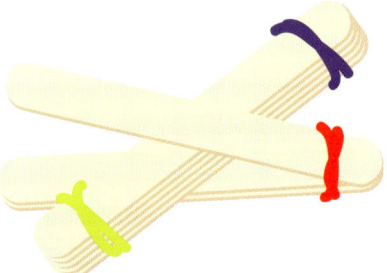

4

Now ensure that the one stick on top, two sticks below and the five-stick band in the middle stay in place.

5

Put a rubber band in a criss-cross fashion on this joint to ensure this as shown.

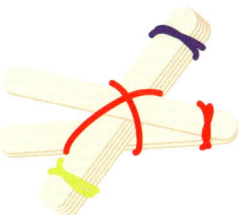

6

Use a rubber band to fix the plastic spoon on one end of the single top stick as shown.

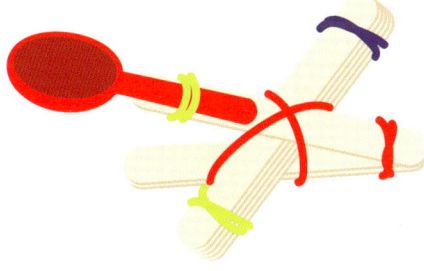

7

Make sure all the rubber bands are tight.

8

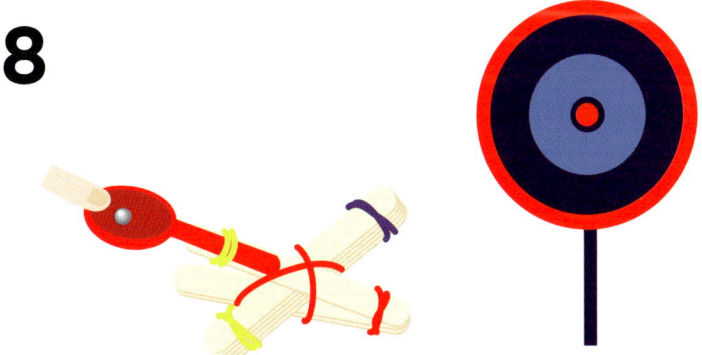

Push the spoon down. Place your ammunition in the spoon and release it to fire away at the target!

DID YOU KNOW?

The working of a catapult is modelled on the working of a common simple machine called 'lever'. A lever is basically used to move something. It is a long stick that you push or pull against a point called fulcrum.

There are different types of levers and our catapult falls into a category called 'class-3 lever'. This type of lever has a fulcrum at one end of the stick; you push on the middle and the weight (ammunition) is at the other end of the stick.

The other levers we use everyday are simple things such as a see-saw in the park, scissors and staplers, even a brake on your bicycle! Did you realize that all these mechanisms have a long stick that you push or pull against a fulcrum?

In designing effective and efficient lever mechanisms, you need to pay special attention to the position of the fulcrum. If the fulcrum is positioned correctly, your lever will be able to work more efficiently and will be able to move more load with less effort.

Do you realize that our body movements also make effective use of the lever mechanism? Imagine your elbow as a fulcrum

Seesaw Lever

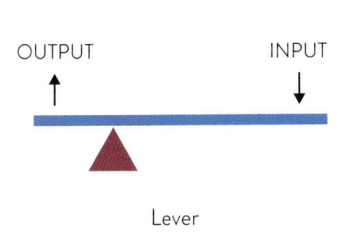

Lever

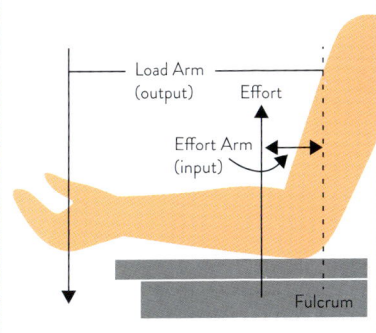

Human Arm Lever

BRAIN STORM

- Adjust the position of the sticks in your catapult so that your ammunition can:

  - Fly higher

  - Fly farther

  - Fly in a particular direction

- Try and build a similar catapult using other materials so that heavier weights can be flung from one end to another!

TRIVIA

and observe how you use it while lifting heavy things or pushing something. Your fingers are good levers, too. As an interesting example—when you are playing drums, you are using an entire system of levers using your drumsticks, fingers and arms!

- Steam catapults are used in naval carriers to launch airplanes!

- The most ancient catapults were known as the katapaltai, which were arrow-firing machines. They were invented around 350 BCE and were used in siege warfare. Alexander the Great said to be the first to use them for cover fire, essentially introducing artillery to the military world.

THE FUTURE WORLD OF MACHINES

A car that drives itself. A vacuum cleaner that cleans the house on its own every day. How about a smart school bag that follows you around by wheeling itself? Or a robot that makes your bed and cleans your room every morning?

Sound like scenes from a science fiction movie or a dream come true? Well, it's turning into reality faster than you think.

SMART MACHINES

The brain learns from experiences and stores knowledge and instructions as memory. It controls the way your body moves—where your legs take you and what your hands do. Your brain has been learning how to do things and storing that information since the time you were a baby. A machine can have legs and arms that move using motors, pulleys and wheels, but that does not make it intelligent enough to learn how to do things on its own. This artificial intelligence can be added by using tiny chips and microcontrollers. These electronic components can store information which becomes the memory of the machine. The components can also store sets of instructions called programs, a sort of training manual for a certain task. Thus, intelligent machines can perform these operations on their own without any intervention or inputs from human beings!

SENSORS AND AUTOMATION

Our super complex human brain is also in constant interaction with its environment. For example, your ears hear the school bell ring and your eyes see the time and that is how the brain knows it is time to go home. It then instructs your legs to move and your hands to pick up your bag.

Just as we have sensory organs that take inputs from the environment and pass them on to the brain, machines use sensors to sense environmental factors such as light, temperature, pressure, sound, etc. For example, a smart car can sense the level of light and switch on its headlights automatically. It can also sense obstacles while parking and reversing. Sensors and programmable microcontrollers have opened up a whole new world of possibilities in machine automation and artificial intelligence.

ROBOTS—MOVERS & SHAKERS!

The machines of the future will be smarter, smaller, more efficient and more intelligent than ever. There are already robots helping doctors with precision in surgery, industrial robots performing repetitive tasks with accuracy, home robots easing our workload, office robots helping us work efficiently. Tiny bots can go inside our body to fix problems and they can also travel in hazardous conditions under the sea or up in the atmosphere to collect data. They may well be our greatest helpers in the future.

DESIGN
THE FUTURE

Now that you know all about the mechanisms that drive machines, what kind of future machine would you like to design?

BRAINSTORM
Imagine you have a secret treasure hidden in your room. You need to guard it even when you are not in the room.

Draw and design a robot that will:

1. Guard the room while you are away and lock it down if anyone tries to enter it.

2. Send you an alarm when you are in the room and someone approaches.

3. Keep the room clean, neat and tidy!

STRUCTURES

'The higher your structure is to be,
the deeper must be its foundation.'
SAINT AUGUSTINE

What comes to your mind when you hear the word 'structures'? Here's what we came up with:

- Buildings
- Igloos
- Bridges
- Floating boathouses
- Pyramids
- Treehouses

The list is endless. Now go back to your history lesson on ancient monuments. Which one do you think has the coolest structure? The Taj Mahal with its lovely domes and minarets? Or the Greek Parthenon with its strong pillars? Or the winding, seemingly endless Great Wall of China? Yes, that's a structure too! All of these are examples of man-made structures. Can you think of some more? What are their special features?

One can also find countless examples of beautiful well-crafted structures in nature, the greatest inventor of all. Think about a flower or a fruit. A flower consists of different whorls that protect the delicate parts inside and add to its beauty. These whorls are systematic arrangements of sepals, petals and stamens. They are strong and brightly coloured in order to attract insects and other pollinators. Similarly, the structure of a fruit with layers of flesh and skin is designed to protect the seed that is inside.

Can you think of other interesting natural structures?

A structure is a logical arrangement of various parts designed to enhance usefulness and appearance. Even something as minuscule as an atom has a structure containing components organized in a specific way. Every single thing—from a tiny snowflake to a gigantic mountain, even the earth itself—has its own specific structure. A good structure aids in effective functioning.

The Leaning Tower of Pisa

Buildings and bridges are fascinating structures to tickle an inventive brain, and you can be very creative while designing them. You can make them stronger, yet lighter, cheaper, more long-lasting, and more eco-friendly. Through the history of human civilization, designing and building good structures has been a major occupation. Innovations and inventions in the area of building technology, equipment and material have only helped make better structures.

Sydney Harbour Bridge

THE STRUCTURAL INVENTOR

Gustave Eiffel

The Eiffel Tower in Paris and the Statue of Liberty in New York are both iconic structures. What do they have in common? Gustave Eiffel. During his brilliant career as a constructor, Eiffel pioneered a number of developments in metal structural work. He built many famous bridges, viaducts and buildings across the world.

He conceptualized and tried out different ways of building strong structures. This spirit of innovation helped him turn into reality many megastructures such as the Eiffel Tower and the Statue of Liberty—structures that most people could only dream of! After retirement, he devoted his time to research in the fields of meteorology and aerodynamics.

He built the first wind tunnel, which was used to investigate the functions of various airfoil sections that were built by early pioneers of aviation. His work in this field helped advance the aviation industry.

As you can see, an investigative and inventive mind is never limited by one area of subject knowledge. Knowledge is infinite and so are the possibilities of invention!

BATTLE OF THE SHAPES

Have you ever observed that every thing has a certain shape? Shapes define everything that we see and use. How many shapes do you know of? Are any of them good for building structures? Let's find out!

MATERIALS

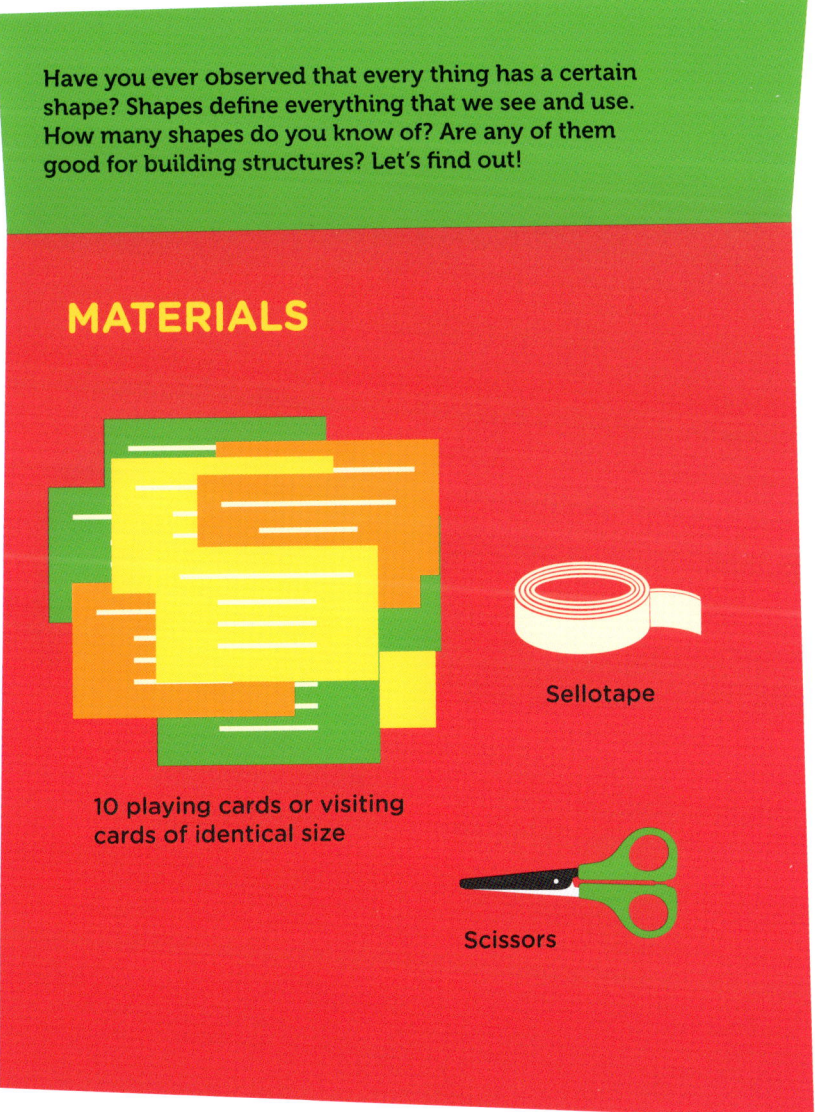

10 playing cards or visiting cards of identical size

Sellotape

Scissors

INSTRUCTIONS

1

Tape four cards together using the Sellotape to build a square as shown in the figure.

2

Tape three cards together using the Sellotape to build a triangle.

3

Stick three cards together using the Sellotape to build an arch as shown in the figure.

4

Press each shape down from the top with your index finger to test the strength and stability of the shape.

5

You can also stretch and compress each shape to check its stability.

DID YOU KNOW?

Shapes are an important aspect of design. Have you ever seen a triangular bed or a square wheel or a circular floor tile? Each shape has its own unique set of characteristics and uses.

Shape is integral to the functionality of a product as well as to its usability, cost and look. When it comes to designing structures, it is important to analyse how different shapes handle the forces that act on them. Typically, the following forces act on any structure:

Tension: This is created when two ends of a structure are stretched or pulled apart. For example, in a beam bridge, the beam is fixed on two piers at two ends and the force of tension acts on the beam when there is a load on the bridge.

Compression: This is created when two ends of a structure are pushed towards each other. For example, any load-bearing wall in a building experiences the force of compression. There are several other forces that act on structures. Some of these are stress, bending and torsion.

In the activity in the previous page, you would have realized that the triangle doesn't lose its shape easily. This makes it a good shape to add strength to any structure. Did you find it difficult to make your square stand upright? Yes, right? This is due to various forces such as tension and compression that deform the shape.

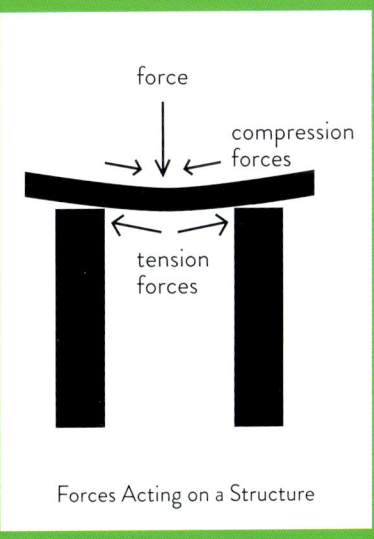

Forces Acting on a Structure

You would have also realized that the arch stands easily. Its shape is designed in a manner that distributes the forces evenly all across.

Good structural design accounts for the characteristics of different shapes and includes them appropriately in suitable places. Hence, all wheels are circular, all balls are spherical and all pipes are cylindrical!

BURJ AL ARAB

BRAIN STORM

- Try constructing different kinds of shapes and test their characteristics.

- Try making a mini-bridge by putting together multiple pieces of the same shape.

TRIVIA

- The Burj Al Arab is a luxury hotel in Dubai. It is the fourth tallest hotel in the world. What's so special about it? Well, the shape of the hotel is like the sail of a ship!

- The shape of the human DNA is like that of an intertwined ladder known as the double helix!

BRIDGE CONTEST

Imagine you're stuck on one side of the river and need to get to the other. How in the world are you going to do that? Can you fly? Obviously not. Can you build a bridge? Now that's a real possibility!

MATERIALS

20 one-rupee coins

12 books (A4-sized, having 200 or more pages)

10 A4-size sheets of paper

INSTRUCTIONS

1

Use an A4 sheet to make a bridge between two stacks of six books each as shown. Place coins on the bridge one at a time and count how many it can hold before it collapses.

2

Add another A4 sheet on top of the first sheet and now count the number of coins your bridge can hold.

3

Fold up the sides of one of the A4 sheets and use it as a bridge as shown. Keep the other A4 sheet aside. Count how many coins your bridge can now hold.

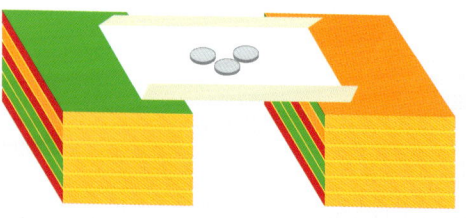

4

Remove all sheets from the stacks of books.

5

Make an arch out of one A4 sheet and place it between the two stacks of books as shown.

6

Place another sheet over the arch as a bridge as shown. Count the number of coins your bridge can hold.

7

Remove all sheets from the stacks of books.

8

Place one A4 sheet in between the two stacks of books as the base and make a fan fold out of another as shown.

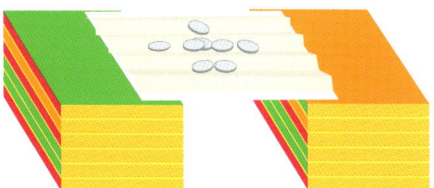

9

Place this fan-folded sheet over the base as a bridge and count the number of coins your bridge can hold.

DID YOU KNOW?

Arch bridge: This is one of the strongest construction forms. This bridge is supported throughout its length by a series of arches and piers. It has been a popular type of bridge for ages.

Suspension bridge: These are modern and more complicated creations and are suspended from tall piers that rise up high above the bridge. Strong wire cables connected to the piers hold the bridge. These bridges are built over huge water bodies such as bays and big rivers.

Bridges are structures that are built to help us cross obstacles such as rivers, canyons, rail-tracks, etc. Bridges have to be strong and balanced structures. They can be built in different ways. The important types of bridges are:

Beam bridge: This is the most basic design of a bridge. It is fundamentally a long plank or beam across the river, supported on both ends by piers.

Beam Bridge

Arch Bridge

Suspension Bridge

While planning your bridge, you need to consider the following:

1. **The span required:** The distance from one end to the other end is an important factor. Beam bridges with piers only on the ends cannot be too long. They are suited for short spans. Longer beam bridges need piers in the middle.

2. **Load bearing requirement:** Is your bridge just a walkway for people? Will vehicles move across it? A bridge needs to be appropriately designed to handle weight. In the activity above, the fan folded A4 sheet bridge is able to hold the maximum number of coins because of its triangular shape.

3. **Cost:** Beam bridges are the cheapest way to build a quick bridge. You need to weigh the cost against other factors of design such as span, load, material, etc. to decide on the best-suited bridge type.

BRAIN STORM

- Repeat the activity above using thicker sheets of paper and heavier weights.

- If you change the distance between the supports, will the bridge support the same load? Try this and see what happens.

TRIVIA

- The oldest bridge in the world still in use is the slab-stone single-arch bridge over the river Meles in Izmir, Turkey.

- The world's longest bridge is the Danyang–Kunshan Grand Bridge in China. Part of the Beijing-Shanghai High-Speed Railway, it spans 165 km!

TRUSS BRIDGE

What if you have to build a bridge that needs to span a large distance as well as be able to withstand a large load? How would you build this bridge? Welcome to an important member of the bridge family—the truss bridge!

MATERIALS

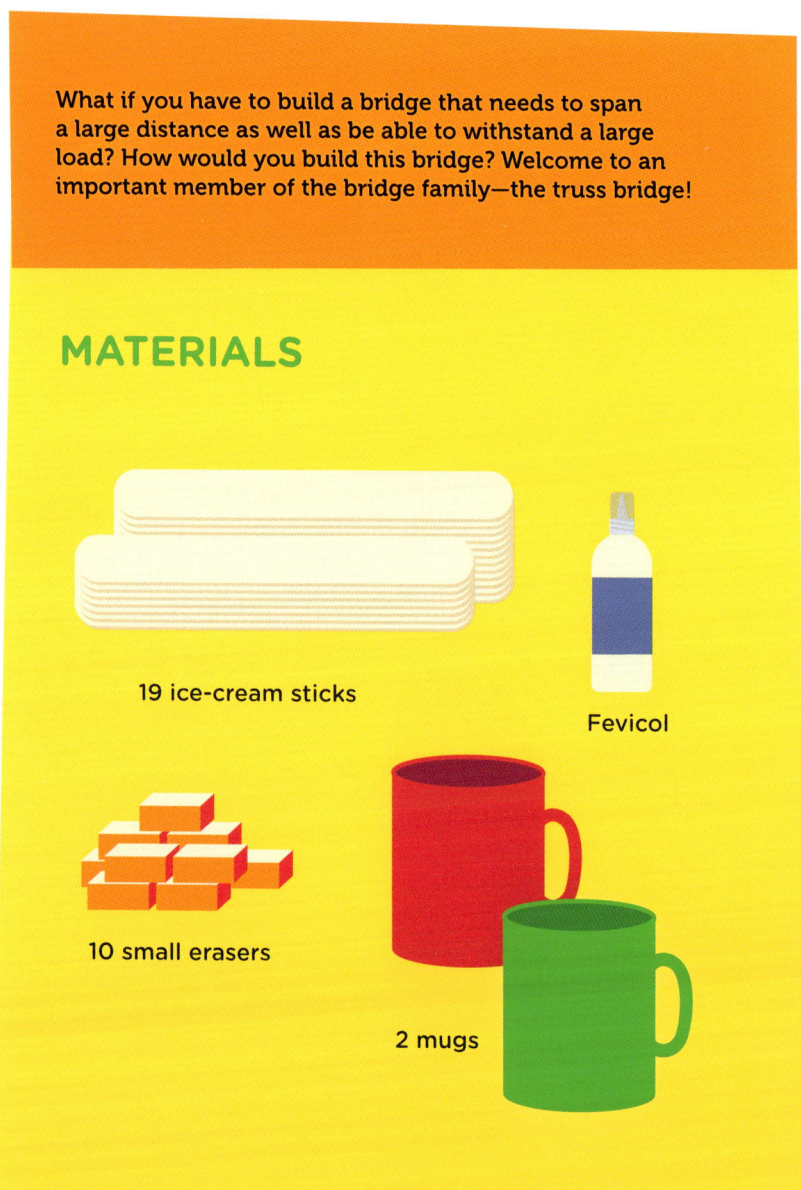

19 ice-cream sticks

Fevicol

10 small erasers

2 mugs

INSTRUCTIONS

1

Place five erasers on a table as shown.

2

Use fevicol and stick seven ice-cream sticks on to the erasers to make three triangles as shown.

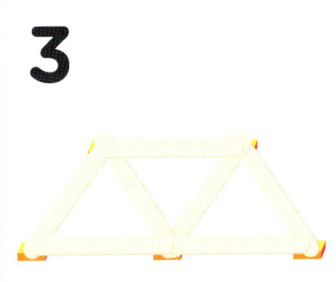

3

These three triangles form one side of your bridge.

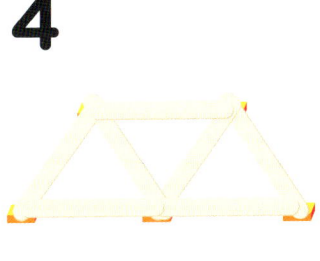

4

Use the other erasers, ice-cream sticks and fevicol to create three more triangles to form the other side of your bridge as shown. Wait for the fevicol to dry.

5

Place three ice-cream sticks next to each other and apply fevicol at both ends of each stick.

6

Vertically stick both sides of your bridge on to three sticks as shown above. Ensure that the erasers are stuck to the sticks. Use the two mugs as supports on either side and wait for the fevicol to dry.

7

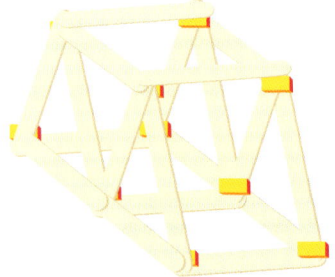

Use fevicol and stick two more ice-cream sticks across each pair of the top erasers as shown. Wait for the fevicol to dry. Your bridge is now ready!

Which is the strongest shape—a circle, oval, square, rectangle or triangle? From the first activity, you must have understood that every shape apart from the triangle gets bent and distorted when under stress.

The triangle stays rigid and that's what makes it the strongest shape to use in construction. The rigidity and strength of a triangle does not depend on the strength of its joints; rather, it is an inherent property of the shape itself. Compare that to a square. When you hold a square shape upright, its top side is essentially a simple beam. A beam buckles in the centre once it reaches its load-bearing capacity. A triangle does not buckle since the force acting on it from the load is carried down to the ends by its

sides. To reinforce a square shape, we need to add a diagonal cross bracing, essentially creating two triangles inside the square.

A triangular truss can be used as a framework for any structure. The truss helps distribute the weight load evenly across different points. This adds a great deal of stability and strength to any structure.

Trusses are popularly used in bridge construction to bear the weight of great loads. Trusses can add strength to any kind of bridge and are also used under sloping roofs as roof trusses. Steel tube trusses are used to support huge structures such as stadiums, airports, etc. Can you think of a fun place where you find trusses? Next time you visit an amusement

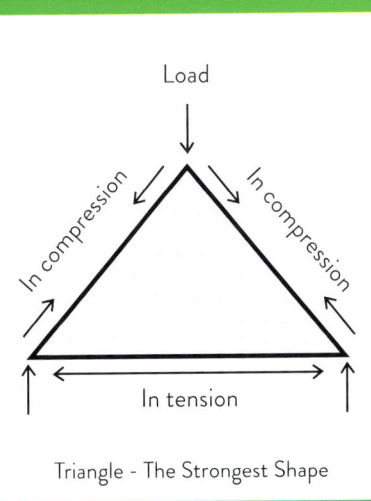

Triangle - The Strongest Shape

Triangular Truss Bridge

park, observe the ladder truss on the giant wheel. The famous London Eye and Singapore Flyer use trusses too. They're what make these megastructures aesthetic, lightweight, sturdy and safe.

BRAIN STORM

- Add more erasers and ice-cream sticks to build a longer truss bridge.
- Place different weights on your truss bridge and measure the maximum weight it can hold before breaking!

TRIVIA

- A cantilever bridge is constructed using cantilevers, which are horizontal structures supported only on one end. With the right materials and engineering, a steel truss cantilever bridge can span well over 1500 feet!
- The Howrah Bridge in Kolkata is a type of cantilever truss bridge.

TOOTHPICK TOWER

Buildings around the world are becoming taller structures. How do you make them safer and more stable? Let's find out using a surprising set of materials! Marshmallows are yummy treats and toothpicks are something you clean your teeth with. Do you know you can use them to make a really strong building?

MATERIALS

1 box of toothpicks

20 marshmallows

A table

INSTRUCTIONS

1

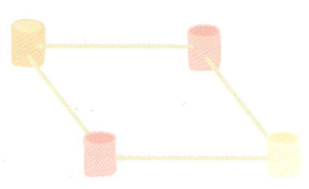

Insert four toothpicks into four marshmallows and make a square as shown (the ground floor).

2

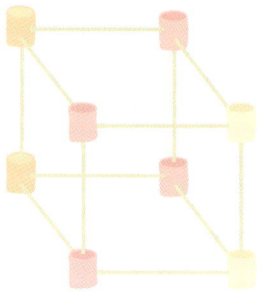

Turn the square into a three-dimensional cube by adding eight more toothpicks and four more marshmallows as shown (the first floor).

3

Add more toothpicks and marshmallows to continue building floors. Build a minimum of two floors.

4

After adding each floor, check if your structure stands upright firmly or wobbles and is off-balance. The higher you go, the wobblier your structure will become.

5

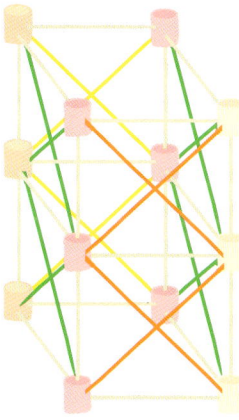

Now add toothpicks across the squares (along the diagonals) to add stability and strength to your structure.

6

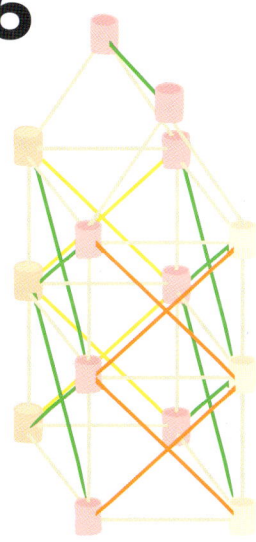

Add more toothpicks and marshmallows to make a pointed roof as shown.

7

Place this structure on a table. Shake the table horizontally for a few seconds and see if your toothpick tower can withstand the earthquake!

DIO YOU KNOW?

above. With the addition of cross braces, the weight was more evenly distributed along the cross section, thus improving the strength and stability.

Tapering geometry is also used to build a more stable structure. This kind of structure has a wider base and tapers as you move up. Remember the majestically tall and tapering-towards-the-top structure of the Eiffel Tower? Shorter structures are safer

Earthquake alert! But where can you run when the earth is shaking?

The only way to survive earthquakes is to make structures that do not crumble and cause heavy damage. How do we do that? In the previous activity, we added diagonal cross braces across the squares, thus creating triangles inside these squares which strengthened the structure. When you shook the table, the building held still because it was fortified by the cross braces. Cross braces and trusses are used to add strength and stability to real buildings. Before the addition of cross braces in your model, did it not lean or bend with every additional floor? This happened because of the pull of gravity and the inability of the lower floor to withstand the additional weight

Cross Bracing

TUNED MASS DAMPER

BRAIN STORM

- Use toothpicks and marshmallows to build a higher structure and test its stability.

- Try the above activity using spaghetti and marshmallows. Is there a difference in the stability when spaghetti is used compared to when toothpicks are used?

TRIVIA

- The world's tallest man-made structure is the 829.8 m (2722 feet) tall Burj Khalifa in Dubai.

- Between the eighty-eighth and the ninety-second floors of the Burj, there is a 730-ton tuned mass damper that sways to protect the building from strong winds and sandstorms!

during an earthquake. Taller structures sway more at the top. Skyscrapers have become common all across the world for the space advantage they offer. One way of ensuring more safety for tall buildings is by using a large weight known as a tuned mass damper. This could be a suspended multi-ton steel ball that reduces the swaying of the building. These buildings also float on systems of ball bearings, springs and padded cylinders. Acting like shock absorbers in a car, these systems allow the building to be decoupled from the shaking ground.

THE FUTURE WORLD OF STRUCTURES

The success of a structure lies in it being safe, affordable and aesthetic. People working in the field of structures—architects, designers, engineers and constructors—are constantly trying to find ways of constructing safer, stronger and better structures as quickly as possible and at minimum cost. Their innovations in building materials, design, building technologies and architecture are making way for futuristic structures.

GREEN BUILDINGS

Our world needs more sustainable eco-friendly buildings. Green buildings:

- Make maximum use of natural light.
- Harvest rainwater.
- Use renewable energy sources such as solar, wind and biogas.
- Keep the temperature requirements to a minimum with clever use of insulation in the building material.
- Do not use harmful chemicals in the building material or in the paints.
- Use local material as much as possible to reduce the carbon footprint of construction.
- Reduce, reuse and recycle to the maximum.

SAFER BUILDINGS

A safety innovation under development is the air cushion that makes a structure levitate during an earthquake. Just as an airbag in a car inflates as soon as it senses a heavy jolt, this air cushion under the structure inflates as soon as a tremor is felt. If properly developed, this feature would be a boon in earthquake-prone areas.

INNOVATIVE BUILDING MATERIALS

What kind of crazy, cutting-edge building materials do you want to see in the future? How about self-repairing cement that can take care of cracks on the road by itself? Or a tile that lights up when you step on it at night? Believe it or not, these materials are being developed in research labs now and will change the way structures are built, felt and seen in the future.

TRANSLUCENT CONCRETE

Imagine a transparent/translucent wall that is as strong as a regular concrete block wall! An innovative mix of fiber optical strands in the concrete block makes it possible. This mix creates transparent bricks that allow light to pass through, thus creating a 'transparent wall' effect!

RECYCLED INSULATION

Can you think of a good use for your old, faded jeans? How about using them as roof insulation? Old denims can be converted into soft fiber blocks and used for insulating the roof!

ELECTRIFIED WOOD

Get rid of wires everywhere! Electrified wood has metal layers inside which make it possible to get electricity from wooden furniture anywhere and that too wirelessly!

NEW BUILDING TECHNOLOGIES

Can a bridge fit into a backpack? Bridge-in-a-Backpack uses inflatable carbon fiber tubes that can be inflated at the construction site. They are then stiffened with a special resin and filled with concrete and overlaid with a deck. That's it, a bridge stronger than steel is ready!

DESIGN THE FUTURE

Now that you know a little more about structures, spend a few minutes designing your own futuristic structure right here.

BRAINSTORM

Design, draw and build a square truss bridge that can hold a weight of five kg or more.

DESIGN

'Design is not just what
it looks like and feels like.
Design is how it works.'
STEVE JOBS

INTRODUCTION

Do you have a favourite pen, mug or a pair of jeans perhaps? What makes that object the one you most prefer? It could be the comfortable grip of the pen, the cheerful colours of the mug, or the way your jeans fit and feel. Colour, shape, pattern, material and size are all components of design that can make or break your impression of an object. Design determines every aspect of your interaction and experience with an object. Design is that all—encompassing function that brings art and science together!

Think of a pencil box. How would you design a good pencil box? It should hold pencils, pens, erasers, sharpeners and maybe a small ruler. Does it need to be segregated into compartments? Would you like a particular colour or maybe a favourite character printed on the box? Would you like special features like a lock and a key or a secret hidden section or a tiny light in it?

A good designer pays attention to all these factors and comes up with a design to satisfy all the requirements at minimum cost and with maximum satisfaction. The focus of a good design is always on what the end user needs and wants.

How do you create a successful and effective design? Your starting point should be the systematic process of design as given here:

1. Understand and define the need/ problem/requirement clearly:
- Talk to the person using the product.
- Observe the situations in which the person will use the product.

2. Design a possible solution and sketch it to help you visualize it:
- Draw the design on paper in as much detail as possible.
- List a step-by-step process of how you plan to make your product.

5. Test, use and redesign to improve the product:
- Test out the model yourself. Ask your customer to try it out and give you feedback.
- Redesign and improve if required.

4. Build a working prototype :
- Follow your step-by-step plan to make the product. Being careful and meticulous will ensure its smooth functioning.

3. Select and collect the right materials:
- List all the possible and suitable materials. Then, evaluate and select your materials on the basis of availability and cost.
- Collect all the required material in one place before you start making the product.

It sounds like an exciting process, doesn't it? So let's take up some design challenges, young inventor-designers!

THE INVENTOR DESIGNER

Adolf Dassler

Have you ever paid attention to the design of a sports shoe? A soft cushion to support the heel, a strong exterior to make it durable, laces and straps for a perfect fit, the treaded sole and studs to provide the right grip—it takes a lot to make a medal-winning sports shoe! Adolf Dassler, also known as Adi, was the founder of one of the world's largest athletic shoe manufacturers, Adidas. His father worked in a shoe factory and Adi was trained as a cobbler. His mother was a laundress and young Adi started designing and making shoes in the back room of his mother's wash house. He achieved great success with his path-breaking designs and innovative ideas. Adidas shoes became world famous when athletes won Olympic gold medals wearing them.

This paragraph from a 1954 newspaper (*Daily Sketch*, 30 November 1954) highlights the importance of design in Dassler's shoe:

'Dassler shoe, a German speciality, is only half the weight of the orthodox English football boot. Special features of the German boot are the screw-in studs which can be adapted to ground conditions, cut-away ankles, front lacing almost right down the front of the boot, a soft toe and foam rubber interior.'

Dassler's shoes became famous for their great design because of the attention he paid to the needs of sportsmen and the game they played. Attention to detail and understanding the user—aren't these good tips to remember when designing your own products?

TOOTHBRUSH TROUBLE

This is a story of three girls sharing a bathroom in a hostel. They don't have enough counter space in the bathroom for separate toothbrush holders. They don't want to share one toothbrush holder either. Let's come up with a creative solution using what is available to us and help them out!

MATERIALS

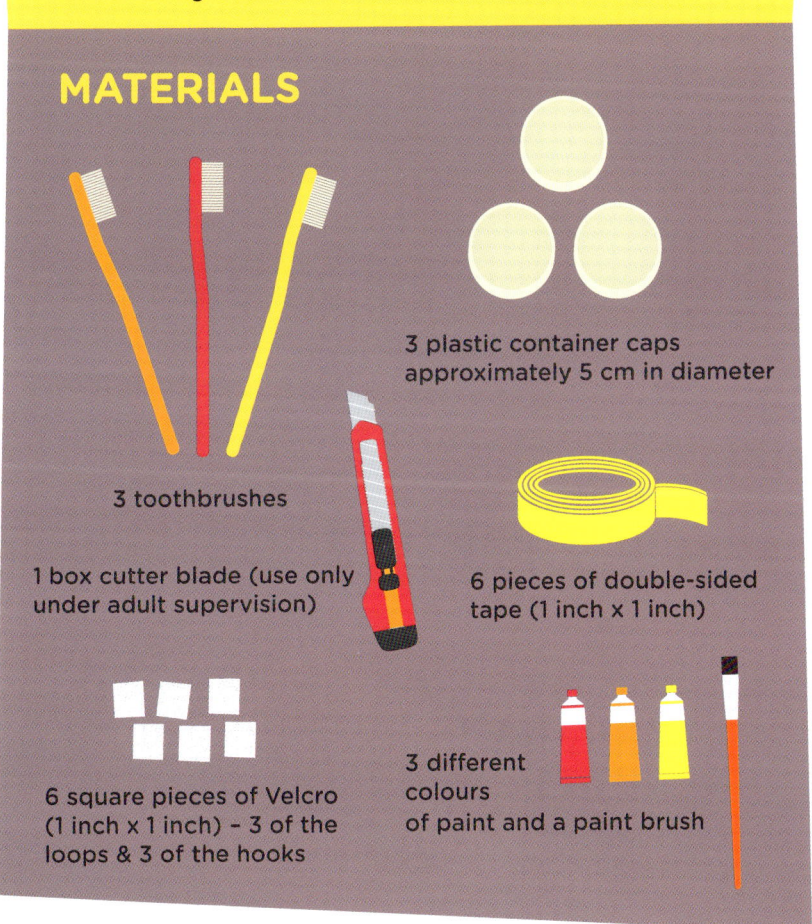

3 plastic container caps approximately 5 cm in diameter

3 toothbrushes

1 box cutter blade (use only under adult supervision)

6 pieces of double-sided tape (1 inch x 1 inch)

6 square pieces of Velcro (1 inch x 1 inch) – 3 of the loops & 3 of the hooks

3 different colours of paint and a paint brush

INSTRUCTIONS

1

Using the blade, cut a slit into each bottle cap as shown. Ensure that the width of the slit is just the right size to hold the neck of your toothbrush.

2

Paint each cap in a different colour.

3

Use the double-sided tape to stick the flat side of the Velcro (loops) to each of the caps as shown.

4

Use the double-sided tape and stick the flat side of the other Velcro hooks to your bathroom wall.

5

Insert your toothbrushes into each of the caps, and stick your caps on to the wall Velcros as shown. Voila! The toothbrush problem is now resolved.

this activity—the Velcro-which was the brainchild of Georges de Mestral, a Swiss engineer. The inspiration for this came from a seed called the **burdock burr** that stuck all over his trousers legs and his dog's fur when they walked in the woods. After nearly eight years of research (it's not that easy to make a synthetic burr!), de Mestral successfully reproduced the natural attachment with two strips of fabric, one with thousands of tiny hooks and another with thousands of tiny loops. He named his invention Velcro, a combination of the words 'velvet'

Some designs are so simple and yet so effective that we don't notice how important the design aspect is. Let's think about the toothbrush. Every morning, you use it while you are half asleep without ever thinking too much about how and why it works. And yet it always does its job! The modern toothbrush evolved from twig chew-sticks and boar-hair bristles. It is a very simple and effective design—the handle provides you with a grip while the bristles get into the gaps between your teeth to clean them out. The basic design is so efficient that it has lasted in the same form for centuries.

Think about the other material we used in

BURDOCK BURR

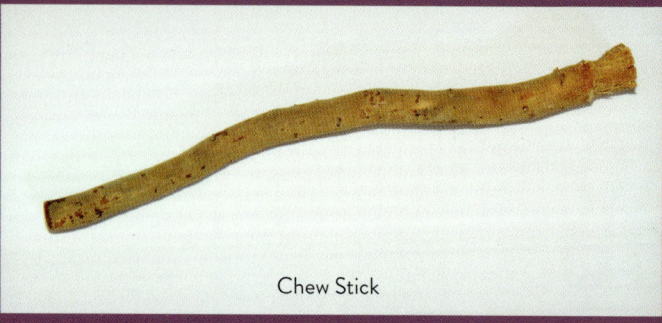

Chew Stick

and 'crochet' and formally patented it in 1955. Since then, Velcro has been the fastener of choice, from NASA spaceships to medical instruments to shoes and bags! It is so omnipresent in our lives that we don't notice the brilliance in the simplicity of its design.

BRAIN STORM

- Just like Velcro, we use many other things to fasten or hold two things together, such as nuts and bolts, hinges, clamps and clasps, magnetic buttons, laces etc. Try building your toothbrush holder without using Velcro.

- Just like the toothbrush holder, can you make holders for your stationery items or keys?

TRIVIA

- NASA uses Velcro solutions to keep astronauts' dinner plates from floating around in zero-gravity space.

- Buttons on clothes were invented long before someone thought of buttonholes to put them through! Buttons were merely decorations on clothes until they turned into nifty fasteners paired with buttonholes!

DRAWER ORGANIZER

Generally speaking, drawers are great big black holes that swallow assorted stuff, never to give it back! For example, what would you find in your dad's desk drawer at home? Keys and cards mixed with bills and receipts, some spare change, letters and papers—it's chaotic! What would you do to organize your father's drawer? Let's help him out by building a drawer organizer.

MATERIALS

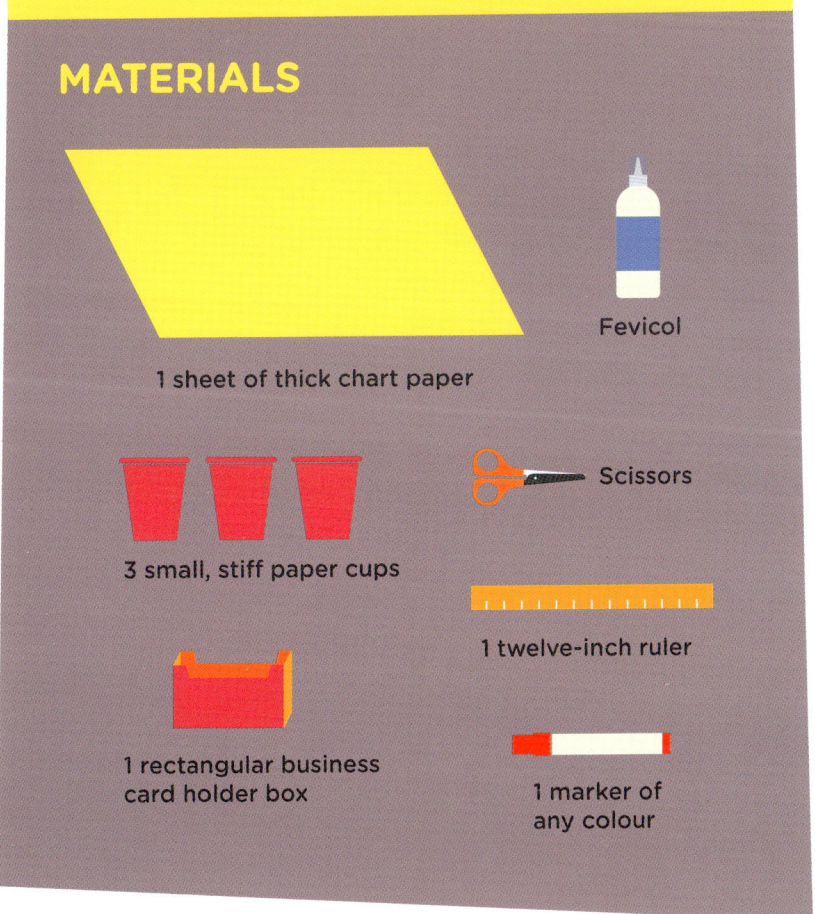

1 sheet of thick chart paper

Fevicol

3 small, stiff paper cups

Scissors

1 twelve-inch ruler

1 rectangular business card holder box

1 marker of any colour

INSTRUCTIONS

1

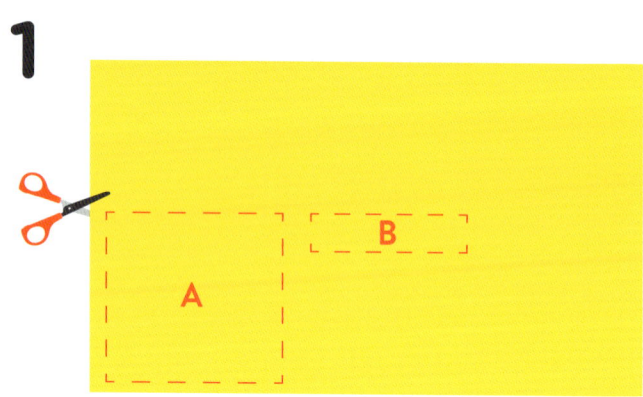

Cut out two pieces from the chart paper of the following sizes:
- Piece A: 45 cm x 45 cm (square)
- Piece B: 40 cm x 10 cm (rectangle)

2

On piece B, draw a 40-cm line lengthwise starting 2 cm from the edge. Fold the paper along this line as shown.

3

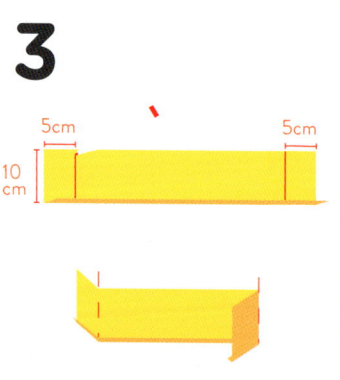

On both ends of piece B, draw a 10-cm line width-wise starting 5 cm from the edge. Fold inwards along the line at one end and outwards at the other end to create a Z shape as shown.

4

On piece B, cut a 2-cm slit at the corners of this Z shape where the two folds intersect. Apply Fevicol on the folded 2-cm flap as shown.

5

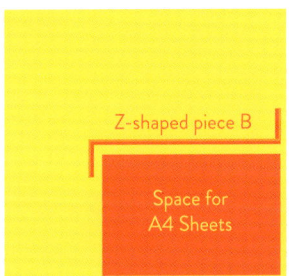

Leave space for placing A4 sheets on piece A. Stick the Z-shaped piece B on piece A as shown.

6

Apply Fevicol on the cups and the box. Stick all of these on to piece A to create storage compartments as shown.

7

Your organizer is now ready to be placed inside your father's drawer!

DID YOU KNOW

may need to sort out stationery like pencils, pens, clips and erasers in the drawer. The kitchen drawer may need separate compartments for different cutlery. Some people might need a sock organizer, a tie organizer or hair-accessory storage in their drawers. Essentially, a product like a drawer organizer can be useful and effective when it is specifically made to suit the customer's requirements.

As a designer, you need to understand the requirements of your customer in detail to be able to design a good product. Who are the possible customers for your drawer organizer? Your parents, siblings, grandparents, neighbours and friends, of course! Every customer will have a unique set of requirements. Your friend

A good designer is able to put themselves in the customer's shoes and walk a mile to see where it pinches! This ability is called empathy or the ability to feel someone else's emotions or feelings.

A good designer can empathize with the customer and understand the problem in great detail

Wheelchair Taxi for the Disabled

KITCHEN DRAWER

before designing a solution. A good example of empathetic design is the extra-large bold print found on the medicine packaging used by the elderly, since they find that easier to read. Other groups like toddlers have an entirely different set of requirements. Men and women have different requirements when it comes to the design of their wallets and purses. The physically challenged on the other hand may need special assistive features in the products and services they use, such as audio assistance, Braille print, wheelchair ramps, cars with extra space, etc. Good design focuses on understanding these issues and solving the challenges.

RECYCLED GARDEN

There are empty plastic bottles—of water, juices and other beverages—lying around all our house. Plastic does not decompose easily. Can you think of ways of reusing the bottles safely? What if the bottles could actually help the environment by turning into a self-watering garden? Let's see how this is done.

MATERIALS

1 twelve-inch ruler

1 piece of muslin cloth

Scissors

1 empty 500-ml plastic bottle

1 marker

1 medium-sized strong rubber band

2 cups of potting soil

1 big spoon

Any 10 plant seeds of your choice (such as mustard or fenugreek), soaked in water overnight

INSTRUCTIONS

1

Use the ruler to mark the halfway point on the bottle. Cut the bottle into two parts here.

2

Take the cap off and seal the mouth of the bottle with the muslin cloth and rubber band as shown.

3

Invert the top half of the bottle and fill three-fourths of it with potting soil using the spoon. Transfer the soaked seeds into this soil and cover them with a thin layer of soil.

4

Fill a part of the bottom half of the bottle with water. Insert the top half of the bottle into the bottom half. Adjust the level of water so that it stays above the muslin cloth.

5

Your self-watering garden is now ready. Wait for a day or two to see your seeds springing up as tiny plants!

DID YOU KNOW?

Have you ever thought about what happens to trash after it is collected from our houses? The food scraps and other organic matter are used to produce biogas which is utilized as fuel. The rest of the trash is buried in a landfill.

We need to minimize the amount of trash that goes into landfills because they occupy precious usable land and pollute the environment around them.

Isn't the previous activity a green use of something as ordinary as an empty plastic bottle? These bottles would usually just go into a trash can and eventually end up in garbage landfills, while you hunt for readymade planters to grow your kitchen garden!

Also, industrial manufacturing is not always an environment-friendly process. Producing anything new uses natural resources and in some cases, leaves behind a polluting residue. When you reuse something, you are saving natural resources,

Process of Recycling

RECYCLED DESIGN

BRAIN STORM

- Can you list ten different ways of reusing plastic bottles, soda cans and juice cartons?

- Try making another self-watering pot using another type of container and see how it affects the design and the look of the product.

TRIVIA

- Recycling businesses—those that segregate garbage and recycle it—generate millions in income every year, literally creating wealth out of waste!

reducing pollution and also saving landfill space. Look all around you and you will find countless things that can be converted into something useful, literally creating the best out of waste! Think of creating storage bins from shoeboxes, pen stands from tin cans, gift bags from newspapers, grocery bags from old denims, lanterns from painted pots and what not! More inventive minds have even converted old airplanes into liveable houses instead of making them scrap metal! Support green design—reduce, reuse, recycle!

MOBILE CHARGING STATION

Mobile phones, chargers, messy wires everywhere! Sometimes, plug points are high up on the wall and the charger wire is not long enough for the phone to be kept on the floor. Sometimes, plug points are accessible, but keeping the phone on the floor leads to a messy tangle of wires. Wouldn't it be better if the charger could just hold the phone while it's charging?

MATERIALS

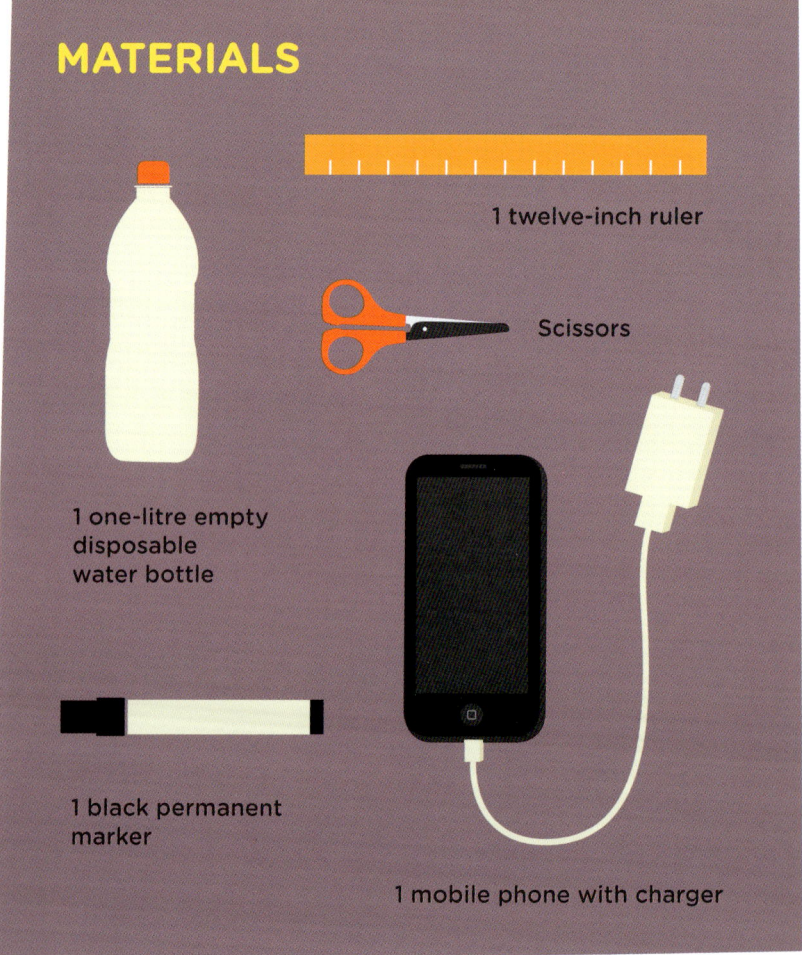

1 twelve-inch ruler

Scissors

1 one-litre empty disposable water bottle

1 black permanent marker

1 mobile phone with charger

INSTRUCTIONS

1

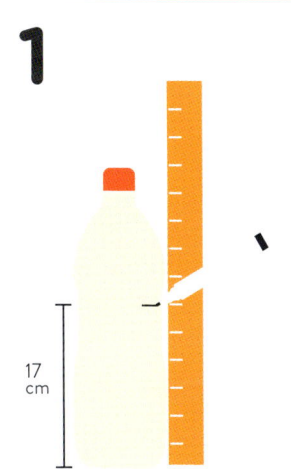

17 cm

Mark a point on the bottle at 17-cm from the base as shown.

2

Draw a line around the bottle at this point.

3

Use the scissors to cut along this line to separate and discard the top part of the bottle.

4

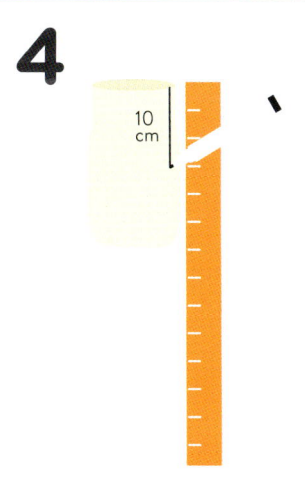

10 cm

Use the ruler and the marker to draw a line 10-cm long from the top edge of the remaining part of the bottle as shown.

5

Draw another 10-cm line diametrically opposite this line. Join their end points to form a U-shape as shown.

6

Cut this curved U-shape out and discard it.

7

1cm
3cm
5cm

On the remaining U-shaped half, starting 1-cm from the top edge, mark and cut out a rectangle of size 5-cm x 3-cm as shown. This is the window for the mobile charger.

8

Your mobile charging station is now ready! Put the mobile phone into the station and plug the charger into the socket through the window of your station.

DID YOU KNOW?

Innovation has transformed the way we do things. Simple innovations in packaging, such as tetrapack material and shape, made it possible to pack and transport perishable liquid food items such as milk, cream and juices all over the world. This was impossible with glass-bottle packaging.

Have you ever paid attention to the flexible drinking straw that you use so frequently? It was invented and patented by Mr Joseph B. Friedman in 1936. It was a simple improvement made to the straight straw by adding a flexible bendable part to it. This innovation made it easier for children and patients to sip from a straw without straining their necks!

Who would have thought that an empty bottle could be put to such innovative use? Innovation means doing things differently. It does not always mean a new invention, but it almost always improves an existing product or an existing way of doing something.

Creativity is thinking of different ideas while innovation is the use of those ideas. Innovation certainly makes a product's design more memorable. Coffee mugs come in countless designs, and you will not remember every mug that you've ever used. But imagine if you saw a really innovative design, for example, a coffee mug that came with an inbuilt cookie holder? Now, won't that stay in your memory?

FLEXIBLE STRAW

Similarly, innovative foldable furniture makes life in a crowded urban apartment so much more comfortable. Innovative energy-efficient lighting solutions save precious electricity. Innovations in communication technology have made it possible for us to see and speak to people all over the world at any time.

You will find numerous places where innovative thinking can be applied. Can you think of an easier way of carrying a heavy schoolbag or of a simple device to clean muddy shoes? Think outside the box!

Foldable Furniture

BRAIN STORM

- This mobile-phone holder can also be used to hold anything from pens and pencils to clips and hairbands to even tissues and napkins! Can you suitably modify its design so it can hold something else?

- Replace the bottle with other household materials such as shoeboxes and juice cartons and remake the mobile charging station.

TRIVIA

- Switzerland topped the Global Innovation Index ranking in 2014.

BOTTLE TORCH

Your city is facing some temporary power supply problems. There are power cuts every night. We need a quick source of light at the bedside. The solution needs to be inexpensive since this is a temporary problem. How do we solve it?

MATERIALS

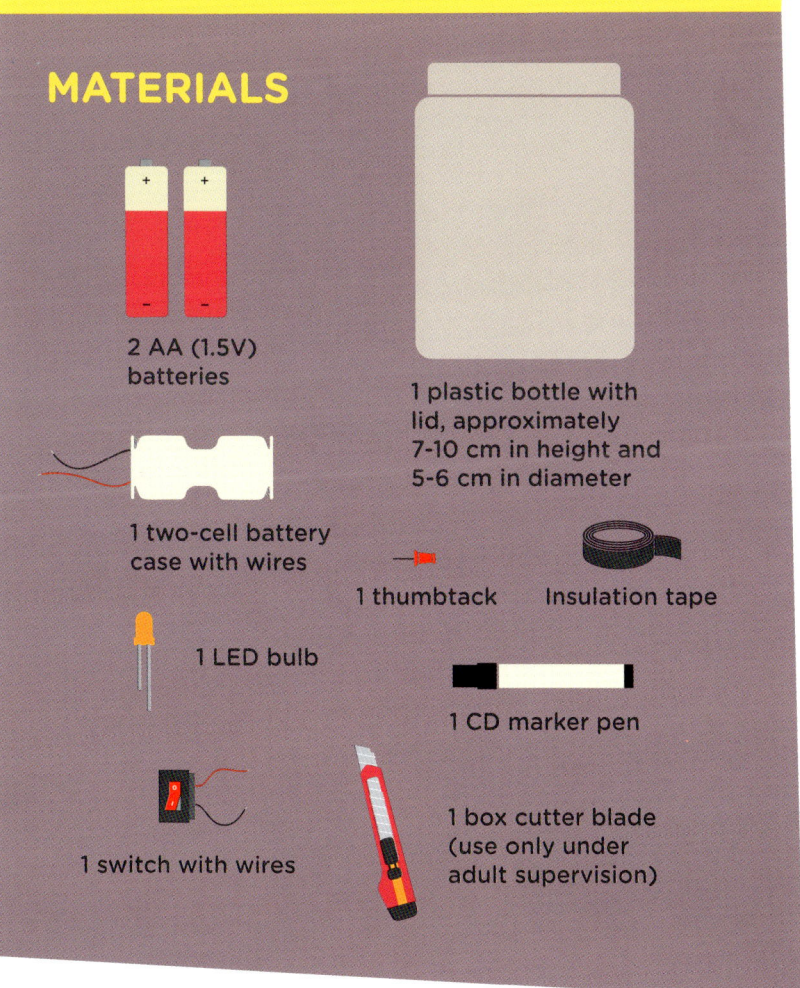

2 AA (1.5V) batteries

1 plastic bottle with lid, approximately 7-10 cm in height and 5-6 cm in diameter

1 two-cell battery case with wires

1 thumbtack

Insulation tape

1 LED bulb

1 CD marker pen

1 switch with wires

1 box cutter blade (use only under adult supervision)

INSTRUCTIONS

1

Use the blade to cut a switch-sized rectangular opening in the central body of the bottle. Insert the switch into this opening as shown.

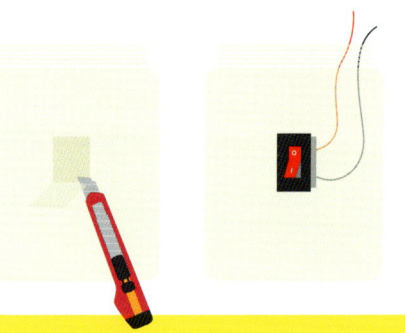

2

Pierce two holes in the lid of the bottle using the thumbtack and label them '+' and '-' respectively

3

Insert the longer lead of the LED into the hole labelled '+' and the shorter lead of the LED into the hole labelled '-' as shown.

4

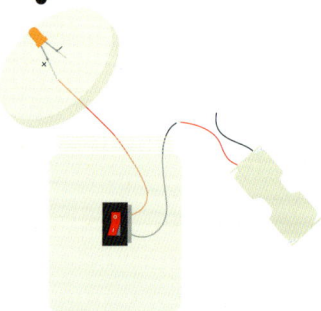

Connect any one wire of the switch to the '+' (red) wire of the battery case. Connect the other wire of the switch to the '+' (longer) lead of the LED.

5

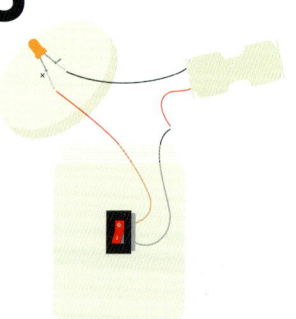

Complete the circuit by connecting the '-' (black) wire of the battery case to the '-' (shorter) lead of the LED as shown.

6

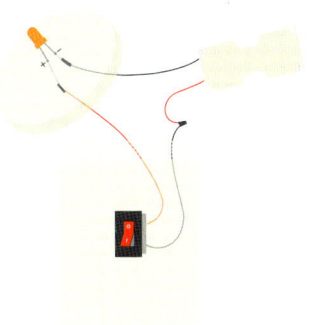

Put insulation tape over each connection individually.

7

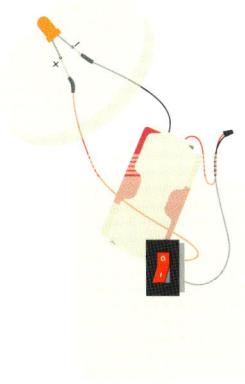

Insert the batteries into the battery case. Carefully insert the battery case into the bottle and close the lid as shown.

8

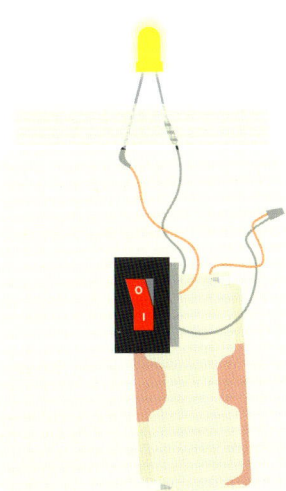

Your portable torch is now ready to be used!

DID YOU KNOW?

What did you like about the bottle torch when you tested it out? Apart from the fact that it works very well as a night torch, did you also notice that it:

- Is easy to carry around
- Does not break

- Is lightweight
- Is big enough to hold the electrical circuit
- Is small enough to fit comfortably in your palm
- Is easy to grip and hold

Did you notice anything else? Although it may seem like a very obvious thing that the bottle torch fits perfectly into your palm, it is actually a very important aspect of product design. There is a science behind making things more comfortable and efficient to use for human beings. This is based on the structure and movements of the human body and is called **ergonomics**.

Have you found some chairs more comfortable to sit on than others? But your grandparents may find some other chair more comfortable. This is because of the difference in the posture and the way your body moves in comparison to that of your grandparents.

This torch feels comfortable because of the way it fits into your palm and the position of the switch that allows for easy operation by your thumb. The same kind of thinking has been applied to mobile phones. These phones fit neatly into your palm and you can easily access the home button with your thumb. The length and width of a mattress, the height of a dining table, the size of a shoe, the

Ergonomic Chair Design

CELL PHONE DESIGN

BRAIN STORM

- In the previous activity, replace the bottle with something else—maybe a soft pouch or an old pencil case—that you can find in your house. Will the torch be equally comfortable to use?

- Try converting your torch into a fun curio like a disco light by using a multicolour LEDs.

shoulder width of a backpack are all examples of ergonomic principles in design. As junior designers, remember to think about ergonomics and make things more comfortable and efficient to use!

Ergonomic School Bag Design

TRIVIA

- The goal of the science of ergonomics is to reduce stress and eliminate injuries and disorders associated with the overuse of muscles, bad posture and repeated tasks.

THE FUTURE WORLD OF DESIGN

The idea of design has been a constant in the history of mankind. People through millennia have been designing and making things. Where is the design process headed in the future?

3D PRINTING TECHNOLOGY

Imagine if you could design and produce your own toys and knick-knacks at home! They would be as unique as you are! Sounds like science fiction? Well, it is a reality today!

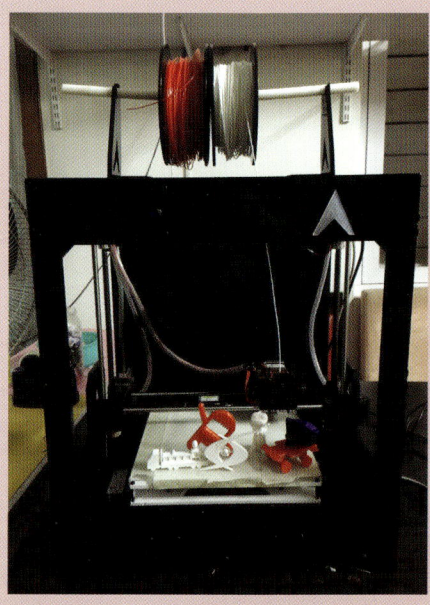

Emerging 3D printing technology is transforming the way things are made. Have you seen a regular printer that prints text on paper? The printer takes the input from your file and deposits the ink on paper, thus printing out the text. Similarly, **3D printing** is a process of printing solid three-dimensional objects from digital designs. Instead of ink, most 3D printers have a plastic filament inside. The printer takes the input from your design file and moves to and fro over a platform, depositing thin layers of melted material according to your design, thus printing it out as a real object!

This technology has made the process of product manufacturing so easy that anyone can do it! You just need to know how to use your 3D printer and how to make a digital design using any simple and freely available tool. As future inventors, you can now turn your invention design into a test prototype in a jiffy!

SOCIALLY RESPONSIBLE DESIGN

With the ever-increasing population of the world and the diminishing of natural resources, the focus is turning towards socially responsible thinking in design. What does it mean? It means reduce, reuse, recycle. It also means maximum use of local material rather than transporting it from afar. It means not harming the environment or other living beings and not exploiting the workers during the process of manufacturing. Next time you go shopping, check if the product you are buying is eco-friendly or not. You can investigate where it has been produced, how far it has travelled to come to the shop, if the packaging is recyclable or not, etc.

DIGITAL DESIGN TOOLS

One does not need to be a trained and skilled engineer or designer to design a product anymore. Digital design software provides all the technical skills necessary to convert a design idea into a technical drawing. Easy availability of tools such as Google SketchUp has made it possible for anyone with an inventive mind and a good idea to try their hand at design.

DESIGN THE FUTURE

Now that you know a little more about designing a new invention, powering it up using a suitable energy source, and making relevant circuits, put all of that to good use and invent an all-in-one lamp that:

1. Can be used as a table lamp and be folded when not in use,
2. Can be used as a portable torch,
3. Uses an eco-friendly source of energy,
4. Uses as much recycled material as possible,
5. Looks like a cool design!

BRAINSTORM

Download and use Google SketchUp to design your lamp before actually building it.

Photo Credits